THE CHILDREN'S PLUTARCH

TALES OF THE GREEKS

ALEXANDER·TAMING·BUCEPHALUS

THE CHILDREN'S PLUTARCH

TALES OF THE GREEKS

BY

F. J. GOULD

Illustrated by Walter Crane

YESTERDAY'S CLASSICS

CHAPEL HILL, NORTH CAROLINA

This edition, first published in 2007 by Yesterday's Classics, is an unabridged republication of the work originally published by Harper & Brothers in 1910. For a complete listing of the books published by Yesterday's Classics, please visit www.yesterdaysclassics.com. Yesterday's Classics is the publishing arm of the Baldwin Project which presents the complete text of hundreds of classic books for children at www.mainlesson.com under the editorship of Lisa M. Ripperton and T. A. Roth.

ISBN-10: 1-59915-162-6
ISBN-13: 978-1-59915-162-5

Yesterday's Classics
PO Box 3418
Chapel Hill, NC 27515

CONTENTS

INTRODUCTION

IT is more a pleasure than I can well say to write of this little book which Mr. Gould has made for the children out of Plutarch's great book. The work is very well done, indeed, with a feeling for the original and a faith in it which no criticism or research can ever quite dissipate; for in spite of all the knowledge of Greece and Rome which the study of scholars has since brought us, the Greece and Rome of Plutarch, which, for the English race, became the Greece and Rome of Shakespeare and of Goldsmith, will remain to the end of time the universal countries, with the "cities of the soul" for their capitals. As I read these wonder-stories which Mr. Gould has so simply, so clearly, so wisely retold, I shared again that stir and thrill of the heart which the Italian poet Alfieri records, with his fine frenzy: "The book of books for me, and the one which caused me to pass hours of bliss and rapture, was Plutarch, his lives of the truly great; and some of these, as Timoleon, Caesar, Brutus, Pelopidas, Cato, and others, I read and read again with such a transport of cries, tears, and fury that if any one had heard me in the next room he would surely have thought me mad."

I should not wish the readers of these moving tales to be quite so violently affected as all this, even when, in later life, they go from them to the same stories as Plutarch himself tells them, which I hope they will be impatient to do. There they will learn much more about the general life of Greece and Rome than they can learn from this book and its mate, Plutarch's Romans, and will see the difference between the two peoples, as Plutarch brings it out by giving first the life of a famous Grecian, and next the life of a famous Roman, and then comparing the two. I think Mr. Gould has done well to put all the Grecians together and all the Romans together, for otherwise it would be confusing to children who did not know their history, and did not realize how long after the Grecians the Romans came. I also like the gentle and right feeling in which he treats the facts, and will not allow any dazzle of glory to blind his readers as to the right and the wrong of the things that happen in the men that do or suffer the things. From time to time he speaks of that awful and cruel crime against human nature, that slavery on which the grandeur and the splendor of the whole ancient world was founded. But he does not, that I remember, make it plain how men and women and children, taken prisoners in war, or even peaceful strangers visiting a Greek city without the protection of some friendly citizen, could be robbed of their freedom and fortune and sold into lifelong slavery, with no more rights than the beasts of the field. I would have had him dwell on this fact, not so as to spoil the children's pleasure in the beautiful and noble things that the Greeks unselfishly did for their country and for one another, but so as to make them understand how in our strangely mixed humanity men could die heroes and martyrs to their country's cause while they lived masters of those whom they denied liberty and country and the ownership of their lives and limbs.

I would have the children who read this glowing book, so full of examples of sublime self-sacrifice, see that the Spartans were heroic champions of freedom in spite of holding the Helots in bitter bondage, and that the Athenians who fell in battle for their mother city could be her devoted children though they forbade their hapless stepbrothers her love and blessing. In such things the Greeks were savage, as the Hebrews were who also bought and sold their fellow-men.

The thing which seems to have made the Spartans so mighty in war and the Athenians so glorious in peace is another thing that Mr. Gould does not dwell on. It was their being, with all the other Greeks, republicans. This made them patriots as no other form of government could; it made each of them feel that he had the same stake in his country that he had in his own home—that his country was his home. Under monarchical governments, where the freeman is still the subject of the prince and not the citizen of the state, the patriot's creed is King and Country, with the King first; but in a republic it is Country first, last, and always, and never Country and President or Governor, no matter how good and great such men may be. Even with our Mother England, where people are as free to think, to speak, to write as we are, and may say what they please of the sovereign, still the cry is King and Country, and men live in the superstition that a king is somehow sacred and somehow superhuman. Their words deny this, while their lives declare it; but in Greece, as long as the Greeks were free, they had no such superstition. They were great because they were democratic republicans and were once as the Americans and the French and the Swiss are now; and I would not have the children forget this. After the Macedonians conquered the true Grecians, and the Romans fell a prey to the tyrants whom their own luxury and ambition and riches had created, all was indeed changed, but it is not such Grecians or such Romans that Plutarch glorifies.

W. D. HOWELLS.

PREFACE

IT appeared to me that, by way of preliminary to lessons on justice, government, political progress, etc., it would be well to create in the child-nature a sympathy for some definite historic movement. With this sympathy as a basis, one could better build up conceptions of social justice, civic evolution, and international relations. I could think of no finer material for this purpose than the admirable biographies of Plutarch; though the national history, or the history of Western Europe generally, would doubtless serve the same end. Western history, however, derives its traditions from Greece and Rome, and it seemed to me an advantage to use a work which not only furnished simple instruction in the meaning of politics, but also held rank as a literary classic. My version is intended for children aged about ten to fourteen, after which period they should be encouraged to go direct to the wise, manly, and entertaining pages of Plutarch himself. The spirit of my selection from Plutarch's ample store is aptly represented in the beautiful drawings by Mr. Walter Crane.

F. J. GOULD.

BIOGRAPHICAL NOTE

THE famous author, philosopher, and educator who is known to us as Plutarch—in Greek, Πλουταρχος—was born at Chæronea, in Bœotia, about A.D. 46. The wealth of his parents enabled him to enjoy a thorough education at Athens, particularly in philosophy. After making various journeys, he lived for a long time in Rome, where he lectured upon philosophy and associated with people of distinction, and took an important part in the education of the future Emperor Hadrian. The Emperor Trajan gave him consular rank, and Hadrian appointed him Procurator of Greece. It was about A.D. 120 that he died in his native town of Chæronea, where he was archon and priest of the Pythian Apollo.

In addition to his most famous work, the *Parallel Lives*, known familiarly as *Plutarch's Lives*, he was the author of some eighty-three writings of various kinds. The *Lives*, which were probably prepared in Rome, but finished and published late in life at Chæronea, were intended to afford studies of character, and the vividness of the mental and moral portraiture has made them continue to be a living force. Historically they have supplied many deficiencies in knowledge of the times and persons treated in his great work.

THE HARDY MEN OF SPARTA

T HE men in the fortress on the hill were so surrounded by their foes that Sous, their leader,
advised them to yield, and they agreed. He spoke to
the enemy from the wall:

"We will own you masters if you will agree to
one condition. For days we have been without water,
and we are dying of thirst. Let every man of my army
drink of the spring which runs by your camp, and then
all our land shall be yours."

This was allowed. But Sous first called his fighting-men together, and asked if any one of them would
forbear from drinking. None would go without the water he longed for. They marched out of the castle and
eagerly drank—all except Sous. His throat was dry
like desert sand, but he would not drink. He simply
sprinkled water over his hot face. Then he summoned
his men and marched off, saying to the enemy:

"This land is still mine and not yours, for we
have not all drunk. Not a drop of water has touched
my lips."

Of course, this was cunning and dishonest, according to our ideas to-day; but the ancient Greeks
and other people thought such tricks quite right, espe-

1

cially if the deceit was done for the sake of one's country; and you see Sous wished to save his country from the hands of strangers.

This chieftain Sous was a Spartan, and Sparta was a rocky and mountainous land in the south of Greece, the cliffs along its shore standing over the blue depths of the Mediterranean Sea. Round its main city, Sparta, no walls were built, the bravery of the citizens being its true defence. Sous was the first man who thought of seizing the men of a certain seaside town of Sparta, and making slaves of them. They were called Helots (*Hel-ots*), and any other captives taken in sieges or in battles on the sea were also called Helots. You could know these slaves in the street by their dress. They wore caps of dogskin and coats of sheepskin, but no other clothes, and each day (so it is said) they bared their backs and were beaten by their masters, in order to keep their spirit humble. Sometimes the Spartans would give the slaves strong drink till they were drunken, and then lead them out before the young men so as to show how wretched and unmanly a drunkard appeared. Yet the Spartans would have fared ill without the help of their slaves, for the Helots were cooks, ploughmen, carriers, and general servants. I am glad to say, however, that no Helot could be sold, and, after paying so much barley, oil, or wine to his lord, he might keep the rest of the fruits of the field on which he worked.

Among the children's children's children (or descendants) of Sous was the famous man Lycurgus (*Ly-kur-gus*), about 825 B.C., who was teacher and lawgiver to the Spartans as Moses was to the Jews. Now, Lycurgus had made up his mind to give the best laws he could plan to the people of Sparta; but, as he knew it was harder to rule men than to rule sheep, or even wolves or lions, he first went about the world to learn all he could concerning people and their manners. Thus he travelled to Spain, Egypt, and (some say) as far as India.

On his return to Sparta, he was made lawgiver; and one of the first things he did was to divide the land into forty thousand small portions, or lots, each being just large enough to keep a family supplied with barley, wine, or olive-oil. And when he passed at harvest-time among the fields, divided into lots, and saw the shocks of yellow corn standing, he smiled to think that the land of Sparta was fairly shared among the citizens, and that each man had neither too little nor too much. No gold or silver money was used; all the money was simply pieces of iron, and thirty pounds' worth of iron would fill a room and need two strong oxen to carry it in a cart; and so it was not easy to hoard up much money, or for a man to become very rich.

Their couches, tables, and beds were all carved in wood in a very plain way, without costly cushions or gilding; and the doors and ceilings of the houses were made of wood roughly sawn, but never polished. Lycurgus would not let the people sit at home to eat dainty meals; all were obliged to come to public tables, and take their dinners and suppers in company. At each table about fifteen persons would sit, and each would bring to the public store every month a certain load of barley-meal, wine, cheese, and figs, and a little

3

iron money to buy flesh or fish. Their favorite food was a kind of black broth. At the tables the children sat with their elders, and folk might talk as much as they would and make jokes, so long as the jokes were not nasty and silly. And if the joke went against any particular man, he was expected to take it in good part, for the Spartans considered that a brave fellow should not only be stout in fight, but should cheerfully stand being laughed at.

The boys had their hair cut short, and went barefoot, and wore very little clothing. They slept together in companies, or brigades, their beds being made of reeds, which their own hands had pulled up on the banks of the river. In winter, they were permitted to spread warm thistle-down on the top of the reeds. When the boys ran races, or boxed, or wrestled, the old men would stand by and watch the sports. At supper they might sing and talk, but that lad was thought most of who could say the best things in the fewest words. The Spartan style of talking was called "laconic," and it was short and shrewd.

Thus a Spartan was asked by a foolish man the question, "Who is the best man in Sparta?" The answer was, "He that is least like you."

Another was asked how many men there were in the Spartan country, and he replied: "Enough to keep bad men at a distance."

So hardy were the Spartan lads that they were proud to bear pain without uttering a cry. On one occasion a boy had caught a young fox and placed it inside his coat. While he sat at the supper table, the young fox began biting him very severely, but he would not make a single sound; and not until his companions saw the blood drawn by the creature's claws did they know how much the brave lad suffered. The girls also would join together in sports, running, wrestling, and throwing quoits and darts; for they took delight in rendering their bodies healthy and strong, so that they might be happier mothers. When their sons went forth to war, the Spartan mothers would give each young man his shield, and say: "Return with this shield, or upon it," meaning, "You must either carry back your shield as a warrior who has fought well, or be carried on it as a dead warrior, who would not allow himself to be taken prisoner by the enemy."

So anxious were the Spartans that all the citizens should be strong and well-made that they carried weak and sickly babies to a deep cave in a mountain, and there let them die. When quite little, the children were often taken into dark places, so that they might be used to the gloom and walk through it without fear. Thus it came to pass that the Spartans were heroic in the day of battle; and, when the question arose whether a wall should be built about the city, the people were pleased with the man who said: "That city is well fortified which has a wall of men instead of bricks." Yet, powerful and warlike as the young men were, they always treated the aged with respect, and, if a weak old man came into a place of meeting, they would instantly rise and offer him a convenient seat.

Some of the richer sort of people disliked the stern way in which Lycurgus made them live, and one day an angry crowd attacked him, and he fled for refuge to a temple. A young man named Alcander joined in the riot, and thought it a fine thing to help in putting down the tyrant. He struck the lawgiver on the eye with a stick. Then Lycurgus stopped and showed his bleeding face to the people, and they were ashamed, and, seizing Alcander, brought him to Lycurgus, and bade him punish the young man as he willed.

The lawgiver took Alcander to his house, and the young man expected a very rough chastisement for his wrong-doing. But Lycurgus merely ordered him to act as his servant, and fetch things for him and wait upon him at his work or his meals; and for several days this went on, the master of Sparta saying no unkind word to Alcander, and in no way showing that he owed a grudge. When Alcander at length went home, he told his friends how generously he had been served, and how noble a man he thought Lycurgus was; and thus Lycurgus turned an enemy into a friend.

When Lycurgus felt himself advancing in years, he made up his mind not to dwell any longer in Sparta. He called the people together and said to them:

"My friends, I am going to the temple of the great god Apollo, to speak with him and hear what he has to say to me. Before I leave, I wish you all to promise me—princes and citizens alike—that you will faithfully keep all the laws I have made, and alter none of them until I return."

The people said: "We promise."

Then Lycurgus bade farewell to his friends and to his son, and set out for the temple of Apollo at

Delphi, and the god told him that the laws which he had established for Sparta were good and useful. The lawgiver thought that, if he never returned to his native land, the citizens would never alter the laws. Therefore, for the sake of the country which he loved, he died beyond its borders. Some say he died in one place, some in another. Some say he died in the island of Crete, and, as the old lawgiver lay sick, he bade those about him burn his body and throw the ashes into the sea. When they did this, his remains were borne by the waves this way and that, and so it was not possible he could ever return to Sparta.

THE WISE MAN OF ATHENS

A BUZZ of many voices was heard in the market-place of Athens. "Is he really mad?" asked one.

"Yes, you can see he is. Look at him now; he is leaping on to the herald's stone; and he wears a cap! Poor Solon; what a pity his brain should give way like this! Hark, he is beginning to speak."

The citizens of Athens crowded round the herald's stone, and listened to Solon. It was the custom for only sick people to wear caps, and Solon's strange appearance made the people readily believe the report that he was out of his mind. He recited a poem which he had composed beginning with the words:

> Hear and attend!
> From Salamis I came,
> To show your error.

Solon was born about 638 B.C., and died about 558 B.C.

Salamis was an island whose mountains rose above the sea on the west of Athens. It was held by the Megarian people, who had taken it by force; and Solon so stirred up the spirit of Athens that the citizens made him commander of the men who should recapture the island. Solon played the following trick: He bade a number of young men dress in long, loose garments that made them appear like women; and he sent word to the Megarian warriors in Salamis that now they might have a good chance of seizing some of the principal ladies of Athens! The Megarians, not knowing the message was a trap laid by Solon, hurried into a ship, landed on the Athenian coast, and saw what seemed to be a crowd of women dancing at a festival. With a shout they rushed forward, but were much surprised when the supposed matrons drew swords and made a fierce defence. In the end all the Megarians were slain, and Solon afterward took possession of Salamis. You will meet many such tales of trickery in the history of war in ancient times; and I fear that in our own days also men do not hesitate to deceive their enemies, and they think it quite right to do so.

In another case of trickery the Athenian people were not so well pleased. The city had been troubled by quarrels between two parties who disagreed as to the best way of governing the State; and a number of men were beaten in the conflict and fled to the temple of the goddess Athene (*Ath-ee-nee*) for refuge. According to the custom of the time, no man might touch them while they remained under the care of the goddess. Some of the opposite party came to the gate, and said:

"Come out, like honest men, and go before the city magistrates, and let them judge if you are guilty or innocent."

9

"We dare not come out. You would slay us."

"No, not while you are under the protection of Athene; and we will give you a long thread, long enough to reach from here to the court of justice, and while you hold that we shall consider you as under the guardianship of the goddess."

So the men who had taken refuge in the temple tied the thread to the altar of Athene, and, while holding it, walked forth toward the place of the magistrates. But presently—perhaps by accident, perhaps by the act of some treacherous hand—the thread snapped. Then their foes fell upon them and killed them. But the people of Athens regarded this deed as a most wicked murder, and later on, when Solon was made chief ruler and lawgiver of the city, all the persons who took part in this action were sent into exile.

Many of the citizens wished Solon to take the crown. They thought he was a wise and just man, and would act as a wise and just king. Solon, however, had no mind for kingship; he was pleased to do his best to govern Athens, but had no wish for the glory of a crown or the splendor of a palace. He found the people of the Athenian country divided. There were, first, the Peasants of the Mountains, poor and hard-working, and always in debt to money-lenders; second, the Dwellers on the Coast, who were neither very rich nor very poor; and third, the Nobles of the Plain, who owned fruitful fields and orchards, and had much power. The poorest folk expected great help from Solon. They hoped he would wipe away all their debts, and they hoped he would take away the greater part of the land of the nobles and share it out among the people generally, as was done in Sparta. Solon did indeed wipe out their debts. He declared that all debts should be forgiven, so that the peasants might make a fresh start in life. Nor, even after that, would he allow any debtor to be seized and put into prison. For such had been the custom till then, every debtor being treated as if he were a wicked person. Solon heard of Athenians who had fled away into strange lands for fear of being cast into prison on account of money they owed, and he sent and brought them back; and all debtors who were in jail he set at liberty. You may be sure the poor and needy folk were filled with joy, and they now waited for him to divide the lands. But this Solon would not do, for he thought it would only upset the whole country; and, for that reason, some who had once praised him began to speak ill of him. Yet most of the citizens held him in great esteem, for they saw that in all he did he sought to do good to the people. Many laws he swept away. Before his days a lawgiver named Draco had ruled Athens so severely that he put to death men who only stole a few herbs from a garden; so that it was said that his laws were written not in ink, but in blood. I will set down a little list of some of Solon's laws:

He divided the people (leaving out the slaves) into four classes: The first class were men who had a yearly income of five hundred measures of corn; they must serve as horse-soldiers in the army, and they could vote at elections.

The second class were men who had a yearly income of three hundred measures of corn; they also must serve as horse-soldiers in the army, and they could vote at elections.

The third class were men who had a yearly income of one hundred and fifty measures of corn; they must serve as foot-soldiers in the army, and they could vote at elections.

The fourth class were men who worked for wages; they could serve as foot-soldiers, and, if so, they would be paid, whereas the first three classes had no pay; and they had no vote, but they could assemble at a big public meeting and shout "Yes" or "No" when the rulers proposed that anything special should be done.

Solon set up a Council of Four Hundred men who would govern the city of Athens. To-day we should call it a Parliament.

He made a law that after a person was dead no one should say anything evil against him.

He made a law to keep the people from spending too much money on funerals. For instance, they must not sacrifice an ox at a funeral, nor must they bury with the dead body more than three garments.

He made a law that no man was bound to support his aged father unless the father had taught him a useful trade. Solon thought this would lead fathers to be more careful in teaching useful trades to their sons.

He made a law that no one should plant a tree less than five feet from his neighbor's garden, lest the tree should spread its roots so far as to draw the goodness away from the soil in the neighbor's plot.

He made a law that no man should keep bees nearer than three hundred feet from his neighbor's beehives.

He made a law that a dog which bit a man should be chained to a heavy log of wood.

For some years he travelled in many lands, learning all he could from the people whom he met. Among other things he heard tales of a wonderful land far away in the western seas. It was called Atlantis, and it had beautiful fields, and its palaces were entered by grand gates, and its people were very happy. Solon made a poem about this happy land in order to amuse his countrymen in Athens. He lived to a great age, and was mourned deeply by the people at his death. I will close this account by a story of Solon's visit to the court of the richest man in the world—Crœsus (*Kree-sus*), King of Lydia.

Solon had always lived in a humble house, and dressed in a simple manner. When he arrived at the palace of Crœsus, he saw noblemen passing in and out, and so richly attired that he imagined each or any of them might be the king; and each nobleman was followed by a train of servants. When at length the Athenian came into the royal chamber, he beheld the king seated on a magnificent throne, and the place was glittering with jewels, and fine carpets lay on the floors, and valuable marble pillars held up the roof, and ornaments of gold and silver were observed on all sides. Solon showed no joy at these sights. To him they were gaudy and showy, and not at all deserving of praise. Then the king tried to dazzle Solon by opening to him his treasure-houses, where were gathered the most precious articles in the world.

"Have you ever seen a happier man than I am?" asked the king.

"Yes."

"Who was that?"

"A plain man in Athens, named Tellus. He dwelt in a modest cottage with the wife and children who loved him. Though poor, he always had enough for his wants. He died fighting for his country, and his neighbors loved his memory."

"Well, is there any one else happier than I am?"

"Yes!"

"Another? Who was that, I pray you?"

"Two brothers who died after showing kindness to their old mother. She had set her heart on attending a feast at the village temple, and was ready to start when it was found that the oxen who were to draw her in a cart were away in a distant field, ploughing, and could not be brought in time. Her sons, in order she should not be disappointed, harnessed themselves like oxen to the cart, and drew her, amid the cheers of the village folk, to the doors of the temple. They sat at the feast, merry and friendly, and that night they died; and all men loved their memory. You see, O king, that I cannot speak of a man as happy till I know all his life."

Some time afterward the armies of Persia invaded the land. Crœsus was taken prisoner, and Cyrus, the King of Persia, ordered that he should be burned on a high pile of wood.

As the unhappy king was lying on the pile he shrieked, "O Solon, Solon, Solon!"

King Cyrus commanded his men to stay their hands from setting the pile alight, and he asked Crœsus to tell why he called on Solon; and Crœsus told the story. Cyrus thought for a while, and then bade that Crœsus should be set at liberty, not to be king again (for that would not make him happier), but so that he might live an honorable life.

THE JUST MAN

T HE judges sat in the court of justice, and before them stood two men, one of whom was accusing the other of a wrong done to him. The name of the accuser was Aristides (*Ar-is-ty-deez*).

"We have heard what you say, Aristides," said one of the judges, "and we believe your story, and we shall punish this man—"

"No, no, not yet," cried Aristides.

"Why not?"

"You have not heard what he has to say for himself. Even though he is my enemy, I wish him to have fair play."

And because he was always so honest and fair to others, the people of Athens called him Aristides the Just.

When the Persians came over to Greece with a very great army, the men of Athens went out to meet them at Marathon, 490 B.C. Only ten thousand against twelve times that number of Persians! But the men of Athens had more than swords and spears and daggers—they had stout hearts to fight for their homes and their fatherland against the tyrant forces of Persia.

The Greeks chose several generals, each taking command for one day. When it came to the turn of Aristides to command, he gave way to a better captain than himself, for he thought more of the good of Athens than of his own glory; and under this other captain the Greeks gained the victory.

After the battle, when the Persians fled in haste and terror, and much spoil was left behind—tents, clothes, gold, silver, etc.—the Greeks left Aristides to look after all these treasures while they pursued the foe; for they knew his honesty, and they knew he would touch nothing, but keep the booty to be shared by all. How differently he acted from the Athenian who was known as the Torch-bearer. A Persian, who lay hiding in a lonely place after the battle, saw the Torch-bearer approach, his long hair being fastened by a band. Seeing this band round his head, the Persian supposed him to be a prince, and he knelt before him in homage; and then he rose and offered to show the Greek a concealed treasure. It was a heap of gold which he had put down a well. Now, the Torch-bearer knew he ought to acquaint Aristides of this store; but, instead of doing so, he slew the Persian, and kept the gold for himself. The Torch-bearer thought of his own pleasure more than of doing his duty to Athens.

Once a year the people of Athens were asked if there were any persons whom they wished to banish, so that the country might be set free from any men that were disliked and dangerous. Each citizen voted by writing on a shell or bit of broken pottery the name of the man he wished to send into exile. As Aristides

17

passed along the street he met a man who held out a shell.

"Sir," said the stranger, "can you write?"

"Yes."

"Well, I cannot; and I should be glad if you would write a name for me on this shell—the name of a man whom I would like to banish."

"Yes; what is the name?"

"Aristides."

"Has he ever done you any harm?"

"No; but it vexes me to hear people always calling him the Just. I think he must be a vain and stuck-up person."

Aristides wrote his own name on the shell, and walked away. The man took the shell, and threw it into a part of the market-place railed round for the purpose. The shells and potsherds were counted, and I am sorry to say that more than six thousand bore the name of Aristides. For while many Athenians admired him, many others thought he was too strict and old-fashioned. But three years afterward, when an immense fleet of Persian ships was coming against the coasts of Greece, the Athenians sent for Aristides to come back; and he returned in time to take part in the battle on sea, in which the Persians were utterly beaten.

During this war the city of Athens had been almost deserted by its people, who had fled to safer places; and the Persians had blackened its houses by fire, and made its walls into broken heaps. After the sea-fight the Persian general of the land forces sent a letter to the Athenians, promising to build their city again, and to give them much money, and to make Athens the leading town in Greece, if only they would agree not to oppose him any more. He sent the letter by messengers, who waited some days for an answer. When the Spartans heard of the letter coming to Athens, they also sent messengers to Athens. They said they hoped the Athenians would not yield; they would take care of the women and children of Athens, if the men would fight on against the Persians. Aristides was in the city, and the people agreed to give answers thus:

To the messengers from Sparta he said:

"We do not wonder at the Persians expecting us to yield up our liberty in return for gold and silver. But the Spartans are Greeks like ourselves. We wonder that they should be afraid lest we should sell ourselves for the gifts of the Persians. No, the people of Athens will not give up their freedom for all the gold above ground or under ground."

He replied to the Persian messengers, as he lifted his hand and pointed to the sun:

"As long as that sun flames in the sky, so long will we carry on war with the Persians, who have laid waste our land and burned our holy temples."

On another occasion one of the chief captains of Athens spoke to the people of Athens at a public meeting, and said:

"I have thought of a most useful thing which might be done for the good of this city; but it cannot be told to you all, as that would hinder its being done."

"Then," cried the people, "tell it only to Aristides, for he is a just man."

The captain came to Aristides, and whispered to him in such a way that no one else could hear:

"This is my plan. The other tribes of Greece have brought their ships into our harbor. If we set fire to these ships, Athens alone will have a fleet, and Athens will then be leader of all Greece."

Aristides went to the people, and spoke thus:

"My friends, the plan which has been told me would, perhaps, be useful to the city of Athens; but it would be wicked."

"Then," exclaimed the people, "whatever it is, it shall not be carried out."

So you see that, though they had once banished Aristides, the citizens now thought very well of him, and followed his advice.

You remember the Torch-bearer who was so eager to get the gold from the well. He was a kinsman of Aristides, and was the richest man in Athens. When, one day, certain enemies accused him of some offence, they tried to make out before the judges what a bad, cruel character he had. So they said:

"This Torch-bearer is a kinsman of the good man Aristides. He is very rich, and Aristides is very poor. Look at Aristides; how poor are his clothes; he is not warmly clad in cold weather like his kinsman; his wife and children have but a poor dwelling. And here is this hard-hearted Torch-bearer; he has plenty of money, and he will not help his friend."

Aristides was called to the court.

"Is this true?" the judges asked, after these tales had been told over again to him.

"No," said Aristides. "It is not the fault of my kinsman that I am poor. It is my own choice. I have few things belonging to me; I want no more. It is very easy to be good when a man is rich. I would sooner try to be honest and just when I am poor; and therefore I glory in my poverty."

The persons in the court thought to themselves: "We would sooner be the poor man Aristides than the rich Torch-bearer."

When Aristides died, he was still so poor that there was not enough money in the house to pay for a proper funeral. Though he had been a captain in the army of Athens, a leader of ships in the great sea-fight, and a magistrate over the people, yet he had never taken pains to pile up riches. Therefore, the Athenians buried him at the public cost, and also paid for the building of a monument, so that all who passed by might see it and keep the noble Aristides in memory. And so well did the folk of Athens love the remembrance of this Just Man that they gave large gifts of money to each of his daughters at their marriage, and to his son they gave a sum of silver and a plot of land well planted with trees. And for years afterward persons who belonged to his family received kind treatment from the city.

In this way the good deeds of a man remain after he is dead, and make the world happier.

> Only the actions of the just
> Smell sweet and blossom in the dust.

THE SAVIOR OF ATHENS

"LOOK, my son," said an old Greek, as he and his boy walked along the sea-shore, "you see those old galleys? Once they were strong ships that carried fighting-men across the ocean, and now they are worn out; they lie half covered with sand in this lonely place; no one cares anything about them. And so it is with men who serve Athens. After they have done their best, and become old in the service of the city, they are laid aside and thought no more of."

The boy, whose name was Themistocles (*Them-is-to-cleez*), gazed earnestly at the old ships. But he made up his mind, all the same, that if he ever could serve Athens, he would.

And he did. In the year 481 B.C. the King of Persia brought his vast army against the Greeks. So many were his soldiers that two rivers (so it is said) were drunk dry by the army. More than fifty different nations took part in the invasion. From one country came warriors who wore trousers, and tunics covered with iron scales, and carried spears, bows, and daggers; from another country, warriors with helmets and iron-headed clubs; from another country, warriors clad in cotton coats; from another country, warriors clad in the skins of lions and leopards, their bodies being painted half-red; from another country, warriors in fox-skins; and from another, warriors in jackets of leather.

The Persian army drew nigh to the city of Athens, and the people were in great fear. They sent to ask the god Apollo what they had better do; and the priestess who spoke the message of the god replied:

"Trust in your wooden walls."

"What can Apollo mean by the wooden walls?" the people asked one of the other.

"I can tell you," cried Themistocles, who was master of the Athenian fleet. "It means our wooden ships. Let us leave the city, send the women and children across the bay to a friendly city, and there let them stay till we have driven the Persians from Greek waters and Greek coasts. And let all the young men go on board the galleys of war and fight for Athens."

This was done in haste, for in the distance could be seen the blaze of burning villages which had fallen into the power of the foe. Women and children hurriedly scrambled into vessels, and were rowed across the broad bay which stretched before the city of Athens. It is told of a faithful dog that he would not be left behind, and when he saw his master departing he leaped into the waves and swam beside the ship until he reached the coast of the island of Salamis. And there he died, and his master buried him and wept for sorrow; and for hundreds of years afterward the spot on the beach was called "The Dog's Grave."

The sea-captains held a council to decide on the exact place where they should meet the enemy's fleet. One of them was angry because his plan was not agreed to, and he raised his stick to hit the Athenian leader. Themistocles looked at him steadily, and said:

"Strike, if you please; but hear me."

The angry man did not strike after all. The calm answer had turned away his wrath. It was arranged to await the Persian forces in the strait or narrow passage between the island of Salamis and the mainland. The city of Athens was in flames, and its walls thrown down; and a huge fleet of Persian ships, with lofty decks, was forming a terrible half-circle around the Greeks. The Greek vessels were flat-bottomed, and much lower in build than those of the enemy. Each ship was manned by rowers, perhaps fifty; and each carried eighteen warriors on the top deck, four being archers and the others spearmen.

One morning, in the year 480 B.C., the fleets were fronting each other, and the sun shone upon the thousands of flapping sails and on the bright weapons of the Greeks and Persians. Upon a tall cliff that over-looked the sea sat the King of Persia on a throne of gold. About him stood his princes, and men with pen and ink were at hand ready to write down the brave deeds of the Persians in the naval battle which was just opening. The Persian admiral's vessel was very high, and from this floating castle he flung darts and arrows at the Athenians. Many were the Persian ships, and they often jostled one another in the narrow channel. All day long the fight continued. One by one, amid the cheers of the Greeks, the ships of the foreigner were broken, captured, or sunk; and the Greeks fancied they saw lights on the land and heard voices in the air that assured them of the favor of the gods. At sunset the battle of Salamis was ended, and the Persian King and his secretaries with their ink-pots and all his proud princes fled from the shore, leaving the throne of gold behind in their haste. Not long afterward the king was hurrying with part of his army across the bridge of boats that joined the shore of Europe to the shore of Asia Minor. The Persians who remained in Greece were beaten in the battle of Platæa. The walls of Athens were rebuilt. Thus was Themistocles the savior of the famous city.

You will remember the old galleys which lay on the shore. The time came when the people of Athens turned their hearts against Themistocles, and drove him into exile. Some say he made plots against the very city which he had saved by his skill at the battle of Salamis. It is very hard to find out the truth from the ancient books of history, and so we must leave the question alone. Anyhow, we hear that the famous captain wandered from place to place until at last he went over to Asia. This was a daring thing to do. He was in the empire of his old enemies the Persians. At one town, where he was visiting a Persian friend, it became known that he was within the walls. A noise was made, and angry men were searching for him. His friend thrust him hastily into a carriage such as was used by ladies. This carriage was like the sedan-chairs of which you may have seen pictures. Bearers carried the chair by means of poles, and the windows were closed up tight. If anybody asked the question, "Whom have you there?" the bearers would say, "We are carrying a Greek lady to the royal court."

Well, Themistocles really did go to the court of the King of Persia. He had first found out that the king was willing to receive him in a friendly manner. In fact, the king hoped to make use of the celebrated general and persuade him to fight against his own countrymen. So glad was the lord of Persia that he called out in his sleep three times over, "I have got Themistocles the Athenian!"

Next morning the Athenian arrived at the palace gates, and the soldiers on guard, hearing who he was, looked upon him with evil eyes, and an officer whispered as he passed:

"Ah, you Grecian snake, it is a fortunate thing for Persia that you have arrived!"

However, the king was much more polite to the visitor than the soldiers were, and talked to him about another war with Greece.

"What plan do you propose for invading Greece?" he asked.

Themistocles looked very thoughtful, and said:

"Sir, a piece of tapestry such as you have on the wall of your chamber has many pictures on it, and these can be seen plainly enough when the cloth is spread open. When the tapestry is folded up the pictures are hid. Now, sir, I have many pictures and ideas in my mind, but I do not want to spread them out yet. Please give me time to think."

"Very well," said the king; "fold up your tapestry for a year."

During this time the Athenian was generously dealt with. The citizens of one city sent him his daily bread; of another, his wine; and of a third, his meat. Often he kept company with the king in the hunting of deer, wild boars, or lions.

No doubt his thoughts many a time stole back to the dear city of Athens, and he longed to be among his fellow-countrymen once more. When walking through a certain city in Asia he saw a brass statue, the figure of a woman bearing a pot of water on her head. This very figure had been made and set up by his own orders in a public place of Athens. His eyes lit up at the sight of it, and he begged the governor of the city to let him have the statue to send back to Greece. The governor refused.

Yes, I feel sure that the heart of the brave victor of Salamis still beat warmly for his native land. The Persians had assembled a mighty army, and they had gathered a fleet in order to descend upon the coasts of Greece. Then the king sent word to Themistocles that all was prepared, and he would expect him to lead the mighty force from Asia to Europe.

This was his temptation. If he led the Persians and gained a victory, he would receive great reward. But he would never feel happy after he had brought fire and death upon the people of his own land. He spoke to a few friends, and with a sigh he told them that he dared not raise his hand against Athens. And then he slew himself, sooner than do a deed of dishonor.

The news caused deep sorrow in the city of Athens, and the King of Persia also felt sad, for though Themistocles had refused to aid the Persians, he did so for a most honorable reason.

He was a witty man, and I think I must tell you one last brief story. Two citizens of Athens asked Themistocles if they might marry his daughter, one being a rich man who had a poor character, and the other had no wealth, but was an honest and just person. Themistocles showed favor to the poor man, saying:

"I would rather my daughter should have a man without money than have money without a man."

And if any young ladies read this story I hope they will think about it.

THE ADMIRAL OF THE FLEET

"THEY are coming! The enemies are coming! We shall be taken by the Persians; our houses burned; our husbands slain!"

So screamed the women in the streets of Athens; and the children added their shrill cries.

"We will mount our horses and go out to meet the Persians before they reach the city," shouted an Athenian.

"No," cried a young man, who pushed his way among the crowd.

Tall and handsome was Cimon (*Ky-mon*), and the hair fell in thick locks over his shoulders.

"No," he said, as he held up a horse's bridle in his hand. "Come with me, friends, to yonder temple; and after we have offered our prayers there we will do as the wise Themistocles (*Them-is-to-kleez*) has advised. We will go into our ships."

The sound of his strong voice and the brave look on his face seemed to put heart into the folk of Athens and many men, women, and children went at his heels as he made his way to a temple. There he laid upon the altar his horse's bridle, saying that Athens had no need of horses and horsemen just now. She must be saved by the wooden walls—that is, the ships. Then he took a shield down from the wall of the temple, and walked along the street to the harbor. A large number of galleys were anchored there. Soon the vessels were crammed with families carrying such articles as they had been able to snatch in haste from their homes. The women and children sailed across the bay. And that evening Cimon fought among the Greeks at the famous sea-fight of Salamis, about which I told you a few pages back.

Some time afterward the Athenian fleet needed a new captain.

"The man we want," said the people, "is Cimon, for when we were stricken with fear he made a stout show, and gave us fresh courage; and for an admiral of the fleet we want a man that will encourage his countrymen besides knowing all about the handling of ships."

So Cimon was elected admiral, and, in the service of the city, he did many great deeds. He gained much treasure in the wars, and his house was well furnished, and his estate was large. Cimon, however, had no desire to keep his goods all to himself, and he did not write the word "PRIVATE" at his gate. He ordered all the fences round his fields and gardens to be thrown down, so that every passer-by who cared might go in and rest or partake of the fruit. I believe that is quite the right thing for rich men to do, if only they could be sure that strangers would behave with care, and pay respect to the beauty of the garden, and refrain from injuring tree or shrub. Perhaps the Athenian people were more polite in their conduct than many American people. Well, besides this, he bade his servants lay out a supper-table every evening, the dishes being laden with plain but wholesome food, and any poor man might enter and eat as he pleased.

Sometimes you could see Cimon walking in the street in the company of well-dressed young men who formed his guard. An old and meanly attired citizen would pass by.

"You see that old gentleman?" Cimon would say, turning to one of his young men. "Change clothes with him."

Then the young man would take off his handsome cloak and tunic and hand them to the aged Athenian, who, in his turn, would give up his patched and worn garments. And sometimes, by order of the admiral, his companions would slip money quietly into the pocket of a needy man, and not perhaps until he reached home did the poor fellow discover that he was richer than he knew!

"Ah," said certain people, who loved to sneer, "why does Cimon bestow so many gifts upon the citizens? It is only in order that they may elect him to some office or make him a mighty man in the State of Athens."

But that was not the case; for, when the common folk had a dispute with the nobles, Cimon took the side of the nobles. He neither flattered the poor people nor bowed humbly to the rich. When a Persian gentleman rebelled against his king, and came to Athens for refuge, he was followed by spies who sought to arrest him and carry him back to Persia. He thought he could not do better than seek the protection of the admiral of the fleet. So one day he called at Cimon's house and asked to see him. As soon as he was admitted to the antechamber (the chamber joining the room where Cimon sat) he placed two cups, easy to be seen, one full of silver coins and the other full of gold. This was what we should call a bribe. He did not think it would be enough just to beg for Cimon's aid; he made sure Cimon would do nothing unless he was paid for it.

While Cimon was talking with the Persian his eyes fell on the cups, and he smiled.

"Sir, would you rather have me for your hired servant or your friend?"

"My friend, of course," eagerly answered the Persian.

"Go, then," said the admiral, "and take these things away. I am willing to be your friend, and no doubt, if ever I need money, you will always be ready to give some to your friend when he asks."

Thus you see Cimon would not stoop to take bribes. He loved Athens, and he loved his fellow-men, and if he did a service to any he did it because it was a just and generous thing to do, and not because he wanted a commission (or payment) for it.

In the year 466 B.C. he sailed along the coast of Asia Minor with two hundred galleys, and met a Persian fleet of over three hundred ships at the mouth of a river. A battle followed; arrows flew; sails were torn; ships sunk; men drowned; and the Greeks captured two hundred of the enemy's vessels. That very same day the Athenians landed and attacked a Persian army on the shore, and captured many tents that were full of spoil. The treasures thus obtained were taken to Athens, and helped to pay for the building of new walls round the city. Cimon had no wish to keep his share of the spoil, and he spent it in draining the muddy water off from a marsh near Athens; also in planting trees in a place called the Academy, so that people might walk up and down in shady avenues. He thus used his wealth for the public good; and that is what every rich man ought to do.

You may remember what I told you about the hardy men of Sparta; and you know Sparta was a Greek State (or country) not far from Athens. Perhaps, too, you may remember that the Spartans kept slaves called Helots (*Hel-ots*). Now, these Helots were not content to be slaves, and now and then plotted to gain their freedom; and no doubt we to-day should think they had a right to do so; but, you see, in those times the Greeks and Romans and all nations considered it quite a proper thing to keep slaves. Well, the Helots of Sparta were waiting for a chance to gather together and slay their masters. And one day this chance seemed to have come.

Hundreds of Spartan young men and boys were leaping, running, boxing, and performing other exercises in a large building known as the Portico. A shout was suddenly raised.

"Hi! look at that hare!"

The timid creature was scampering past the Portico as hard as it could run. With a great halloo the young men followed after it, laughing and joking. Just then an earthquake happened. The ground trembled; the rocks on the mountain near the city were loosened, and the Portico fell with a crash, burying the boys in the ruins. People were in terror lest their houses should come down upon their heads, and ran hither and thither for safety. In the midst of the terror the slaves were quietly assembling. They had no houses to lose; they wanted their liberty; and they thought now was the moment to strike. When one of the Spartan rulers saw the danger he bade men blow trumpets of alarm, and, at the sound, the Spartan citizens seized swords, spears, and shields, and rushed to the usual meeting-place of the warriors; and then they were told of the peril of the slaves. Even as it was the Helots would not give up hope, but retired to the country, so as to form an army for the assault on the city of Sparta.

In the hour of distress the Spartans sent word to Athens, and begged for help. The messenger was clad in a red cloak, and when he stood among the crowd of Athenians who gathered round him they noticed the strange contrast between the redness of his robe and the ashen paleness of his cheeks.

"No," cried one speaker; "let the Spartans fight their own battles. It is not our business. Sparta has always been proud and jealous toward Athens. Let the slaves make themselves lords, and Sparta will learn a lesson and be humble."

Then stood up the admiral of the fleet, and the faces of the people were turned toward him earnestly.

"It may be true," he said, "that Sparta has been proud and jealous; and that was wrong. But, after all, my friends, Sparta is a Greek State, and the city of Sparta is a companion to Athens. We ought not to take pleasure in seeing the limbs of our friends crippled; and we ought not to take pleasure in seeing the companions of Athens injured."

At that the people raised a great shout, and asked Cimon to lead them to the aid of Sparta; and he did so, and Sparta was delivered from the fear of the Helots.

Years afterward Cimon commanded the fleet of Athens in an expedition against the Persians, and he arrived off the shores of Egypt, in sight of the enemy's ships; but there he fell sick and died. As he lay dying he said to the sailors about him:

"Conceal my death. If the Persians know I am dead, they will attack you with the more boldness. Sail away before they learn the fact."

And the sails were spread, and the Athenian fleet made its way toward Greece as the sun was setting; and the sun went down, and the admiral died. His last thought was for the city which he loved.

THE MAN WHO MADE ATHENS BEAUTIFUL

"YOUR head is like an onion!"

No answer.

"You brute, you scamp, your head is too big for your body."

No answer.

The man who did not answer was Pericles (*Per-i-kleez*), ruler of the State of Athens. Why the fellow was shouting at him along the street in this way I do not know. Pericles quietly kept on his road till he reached the door of his house. It was getting dusk, but through the darkness the voice behind still bawled. Pericles called to one of his servants:

"Bring a lighted torch," he said, "and show this person the way home."

That was all the reply that Pericles gave to the rude Athenian. You see, he was a man of self-command. He did not break into a fury when he was insulted. This was not because he was weak or timid. When Athens was at war, Pericles joined the army, or sailed with the fleet.

He was a great favorite with the people; and you
will not wonder at it when I tell you what he did for
them. Any poor Athenian was allowed money to pay
for admission to the open-air theatre. Soldiers were
paid wages; and every year sixty galleys cruised about
the sea for eight months, and the men who were
trained in these ships as sailors were paid all the time.
Corn was sold to poor persons very cheap. And parties
of two hundred and fifty, and even one thousand, persons were sent across the water to settle in foreign
cities where they would still be protected by the power
of Athens. And if you had walked about the city in the
days of Pericles, you would have seen large numbers of
men at work building walls, archways, and temples,
and using vast loads of stone, brass, ivory, gold, ebony-
wood, cypress-wood, and so on. You would have seen
carpenters, masons, braziers (or brass-workers), gold-
smiths, painters, rope-makers, leather-cutters, paviors
(those who laid pavement down in the roads), wagon-
ers, and porters. Handsome statues of gods and
goddesses were set up in the temples and streets. One
statue was that of the lady Athene (*Ath-ee-nee*), made of
shining gold and polished white ivory; she wore a tunic
that reached down to her feet; a spear was in her hand,
a dragon lay on the ground before her, and two sharp-
beaked griffins grew out of her helmet. Where did the
money come from to pay for these things? Well, I am
afraid it mostly came from taxes (or tribute), which the
city of Athens forced out of other people in the lands
and islands round about. So, though the galleys sailed
proudly, and the statues looked splendid, and the people enjoyed the plays at the free theatres, the glory

could not last, because it was got by spoil from other people. Pericles had the rule for forty years.

The heart of Pericles was generous, and he was ever ready to aid a man who was in want. An old philosopher (or teacher of wisdom) had become so poor that he wished to die, and he lay down in despair, and covered up his head. Some people ran to the ruler.

"Sir," they cried, "your old friend, the philosopher, has covered up his head!"

Pericles knew at once what that meant. In ancient Greece it was a sign that a man would put an end to his life. The old philosopher meant to starve himself.

In great haste Pericles went to the house where his friend lay.

"My dear friend," he cried, "do not die like this. We cannot lose you; you are a man whom we love."

"Ah," groaned the old man, who was a wit in his way. "Ah, Pericles! those who want a lamp to burn always take care to keep it filled with oil."

He meant that if people cared for him they ought to keep him supplied with the food, etc., which he needed; and you may be sure that Pericles did not let his friend die.

Two years before his death a war broke out between Athens on the one side and Sparta and her allies (friends) on the other, and this war lasted thirty years; but Pericles only saw the beginning of it. Sad indeed he would have felt if he could have looked on to the close of the war and seen his beloved city defeated and its walls thrown down. He had fitted out a fleet of one hundred and fifty ships, and had just gone on board his own galley when the sky became dull and the earth took on a strange, gray color. Can you guess what had happened? The moon was passing between the sun and the earth, and so casting a shadow. It was an eclipse (or hiding) of the sun. The Greeks were in much fear, and the pilot of the commander's ship trembled exceedingly. Then Pericles took off his cloak, and placed it over the man's eyes, and said:

"Are you frightened at my cloak eclipsing you?"

"No, sir."

"Well, then, why are you frightened at the eclipse of the sun, which happens to be caused by something bigger than my cloak?"

The pilot regained his nerve, and the story was told from mouth to mouth, and there was no more terror in the fleet.

However, the ships returned to Athens without having done anything very remarkable, and the citizens were angry, and made Pericles pay a heavy fine of money. Before long they changed their minds, restored him his money, and chose him again for leader of the State. But the days of Pericles were soon to end. At this time a dire plague began in the city, and many thousands of the folk died. Some say it was caused by so many people flocking into Athens to escape from the Spartan foe, and these strangers were mostly country persons who were used to the pure air of the fields, and who fell ill when they breathed the close air of the crowded houses of Athens. The sons of Pericles died, and one of these was specially beloved, and as the father laid a garland of flowers on the head of his dead son he burst into tears.

And not long afterward he took the fever himself, and lay dying.

One day his friends were standing about his bed, and he was so still they thought him asleep or in a faint, and they spoke one to another of his life and deeds.

"How beautiful a city he has made Athens; and men from foreign lands come to admire it."

"The temple on the hill—how fine a piece of work is that; and we should never have had it if Pericles had not carried out the plan."

"And how the people took delight in going to the theatres free."

"The isles of the sea paid tribute to Athens because they feared the power of our ruler."

"Ah, my dear fellows," said Pericles, who had been listening, "other men have done such deeds as these. You have left out the one thing of which I am proud."

"What is that, sir?"

"It is the fact that no Athenian has ever put on mourning because of me, for I have caused the death of no dweller in this city."

And thus Pericles died.

Just a few words about the Maiden's Chamber before I finish. This was the temple on the hill that was mentioned by one of the friends of the dying ruler. In the Greek tongue the Maiden's Chamber was called the Parthenon (*Parth-e-non*).

It was built of marble, and was about twice as long as it was broad. Instead of walls all round it there were tall pillars, eight at each end and fifteen at each side, so that whichever way you entered you would pass in between marble pillars. Inside the first rows of pillars was a second row, all the way round. And over the tops of the pillars, and all round the temple, were pictures in stone—I mean carvings. These carvings showed the battles of the gods and the wicked giants; the battle of the Athenian warriors with the fierce women of the North, called Amazons; and a procession of men on horses. If ever you would like to see any of these sculptured horses and men and women soldiers, you need not go to Greece. You can find plaster casts of them in the art museums of New York, Chicago, and other cities, though I am sorry to say they show that the originals, now in the British Museum, are very much battered and broken.

When the power of the Greeks had passed the temple was used as a church, and was named after the Virgin Mary. This was in what we called the Middle Ages (from about the year 400 to 1300 or 1400). Afterward the Turks were its masters, and made it into a mosque (*mosk*). In the year 1587 a war took place between the Turks and the people of Venice. And one day—what was that?

Boom!

A store of gunpowder which had been placed in the temple by the Turkish soldiers had exploded, and the building was almost destroyed.

War is a hateful thing. It brings to ruin the lovely carvings of the Maiden's Chamber, and it slays men who were once pretty babes nestling at the breasts of their mothers.

THREE POWERS

THE conqueror who marched with his Greek soldiers right from the shores of Asia Minor to India, the land of elephants, was Alexander the Great (356 B.C. to 323 B.C.). The god of strength who slew lions and fought wild bulls was Hercules. The prince of the city of Troy, who in valiant combat killed thirty-one chiefs, was Hector. The Spartan general who captured the city of Athens was Lysander (*Ly-san-der*).

Lysander had the glory of ending a war which lasted twenty-eight years—a war between Greeks and Greeks, between the warriors of Athens and the hardy men of Sparta. The war went on from the year 431 B.C. to 404 B.C. On land Greek had spilled the blood of Greek; and on sea, among the fair and fruitful islands, the galleys had sailed to and fro and crashed against each other in the shock of battle. At last the Spartans, led by Lysander, suddenly attacked the Athenian fleet at a time when one hundred and twenty ships lay off the shore with scarce a man in them. The Athenian admiral gave the alarm, and hurried on board with all the men he could find. Others came running from the camp on the beach, where they had been cooking dinner, or taking their ease. Only nine galleys escaped, and a number of Athenians were slain and three thousand were made prisoners. Lysander sailed homeward in triumph, his men singing songs of joy, and the musicians playing flutes. Then the Spartan general turned upon Athens, the beautiful city by the sea. Many people had crowded for refuge into the city, hoping its long walls would protect them from the Spartans. But after three months the place surrendered. Lysander caused many players to sound their instruments—wind and string and drum—and, while the music sounded, the Spartans flung down the long walls and burned the Athenian ships. Such was the POWER OF THE SWORD.

Nine years afterward Lysander laid siege to a town, and one evening at sunset he approached the gates, when the garrison suddenly rushed out and fell upon him and his companions, and he died. Thus Lysander, who became great by the power of the sword, died by the sword.

During the celebrated war of which I have just been telling you, Lysander had gained an immense spoil, crowns of gold, vessels of gold, and much coin of gold and silver; and he sent the treasure to Sparta in the keeping of an officer named Gylippus (*Gy-lip-pus*). The treasure was fastened in a large number of bags, in each of which Lysander had placed a note to say how much the bag contained, such as one thousand silver coins and two silver cups, and so on. Each bag was sealed with wax. Now, Gylippus was a man who was brave in war, and a very famous captain, but his heart was touched with the passion of greed. He faced the swords and darts of the Athenians without dread, but the sight of money made him weak as water, and he coveted the treasure which belonged to his city. On his way to Sparta he cut open every bag at the bottom, took out some of the silver and gold, sewed up the rents, and handed the bags to the magistrates of the city. Since the seals were unbroken, he thought all was well, and that he should not be found out. He did not know Lysander had put a note in each bag. And what do you think he did with the stolen money? He hid the coins under the straw thatch of the roof of his house. And I must tell you that the coins bore the image of an owl, which was a sacred bird to the Athenians, and was therefore pictured on their money. When the magistrates opened the bags and counted the treasure, and examined the figures on the notes, they were surprised to find that no bag contained the right amount.

"How is this, Gylippus?" asked the magistrates.

The officer turned red, and tried to stammer out a reason for the shortness of the money.

Just at this moment the servant of Gylippus stepped forward.

"Gentlemen," he said to the magistrates, "a good many owls are roosting under the thatch of my master's house."

No doubt you understood what he meant. The money was found, and Gylippus was so ashamed that he left the country altogether. Thus you see how this brave man was disgraced because he fell under the POWER OF MONEY.

The people of Sparta even passed a resolution that the money in the bags should not be shared out at all, but kept as a public treasure—that is, kept for the use of all the people, as in paying for statues, buildings, etc. And I think that was a good plan. The treasure or wealth in a nation should be used for the good of all the folk in that nation, and not just for a few.

Again, we read in the life of Lysander that he was rather vain—that is, he thought too much of himself, and was too fond of praise. After he had, as I have related, thrown down the long walls and burned the galleys of Athens, a poet brought to him a paper of verses written in his honor. And the Spartan general was so pleased that he gave the poet a hat full of silver. We sometimes read in the newspapers of a minister or teacher receiving a purse of gold from the people who admire him, but we should not think of handing the gift in a hat. I supposed the Greek poet did not mind the hat so long as he got the silver. Perhaps, indeed, he only wrote his verses in order to secure the pay. If so, I am afraid that would show the power of money over the poet and his poetry.

But I have a better tale to tell you about the POWER OF POETRY.

Not long before the fall of Athens the citizens had sent an army in many ships to attack the seaport town of Syracuse (*Sy-ra-kuze*), in the island of Sicily. The people of this seaport were Greeks, and spoke the same tongue as the Athenians and read the same books, and enjoyed the same plays at the theatres, and sang the same hymns at the temples. The Athenians quite failed in their purpose. Their commander was slain, their ships taken, and the whole army was made prisoners. Many of the Athenians were sent to toil in the quarries, getting up stone; and their daily food was but a pint of barley and a half pint of water. Many others were employed as slaves in the households of the richer citizens of Syracuse. Now the people of the city took great pleasure in hearing the poems of a certain writer named Euripides (*U-rip-id-eez*). The Athenian prisoners knew many of his lines by heart, and could sing some of the verses which he had composed not long before, and which were not yet known to the people of Syracuse. With much delight they would gather round the slave who was about to recite or sing, and they listened with silent attention till he had done, and then broke into loud applause.

"Friend," the owner of the slave would then say, "in return for your song I give you your freedom. You may go."

A number of Athenians who were thus released from bondage went back to Athens and called on the old poet.

"We have come to thank you for giving us our liberty," they said.

"How? I have done nothing for you."

"Oh yes, you have, sir. We sang your verses to our masters when we were slaves in Syracuse, and they showed their thanks by setting us free."

It is also related that a ship from Athens was once pursued by sea-robbers, and tried to enter a harbor on the coast of Sicily. The people at the harbor-mouth shouted out:

"You are Athenians; we cannot let you enter."

"But the pirates are following us. Let us take shelter here, we pray you!"

"Can you repeat to us any of the poems of Euripides?"

"Yes."

"Then come in, and welcome!"

The ship sailed into the harbor; the pirates lost their prize, and a crowd of people were soon gathered about the sailors, listening to lines from their favorite poet.

The power of the sword is cruel. It takes life, and works ruin.

The power of money is mean. It tempts brave men to do low and base deeds.

The power of poetry is noble. It fills the heart with tender feelings; it writes high thoughts in our memory; it makes the eye sparkle with desire to do things that are fair and just. The poet is a friend who teaches us concerning all beautiful things—sunsets, sea, blue sky, and the dreams in the minds of heroes. The poet is the man

> Whose dwelling is the light of setting suns,
> And the round ocean, and the living air,
> And the blue sky, and in the mind of man.

THE MAN WITH MANY FACES

TWO boys were wrestling in the streets of Athens, each trying to fling the other to the ground. One of them was just on the point of falling when he bit the hands of his rival, and made him let go his hold.

"Ho!" cried the other wrestler, "you are biting like a woman!"

"No," he replied, "I bite like a lion."

Well, lions may bite if they please; but it does not appear to me to be manly for lads to bite, even in sport.

The boy who bit had a long Greek name—Alcibiades (*Al-ki-by-a-deez*). He lived from about 450 B.C. to 404 B.C.

One day he was playing at dice with other Athenian lads in the street. Just as he was about to throw the little square blocks of bone a wagon rumbled along, and Alcibiades called out to the driver to stop. The man took no notice of the boy's call, and came on. Thereupon Alcibiades laid himself across the narrow road, and dared the driver to run over him. This, of course, the driver would not do, and he was obliged to come to a halt, and the boy laughed at having got his own way.

When he grew to be a young man he was the talk of the city. He was rich, his house was splendid, his clothes costly; and many persons followed him and courted him in the hope of getting favors and gifts. As a man, he did strange freaks just the same as in his earlier years, and the Athenian folk would tell each other, with smiles, stories of his jests and peculiar deeds. He would not play the flute because he said it made the player twist his mouth into ugly shapes, but he would rather play the stringed instrument called the lyre. And the young men of Athens followed his fashion, and none of them would buy or touch a flute.

A certain man invited Alcibiades to a feast at his house, and prepared a grand meal, setting gold and silver vessels on his table. Many guests were entering the banqueting-hall, when Alcibiades suddenly strode in, attended by several of his serving-men, and he bade them snatch up half the precious cups and carry them away. And they did so. The guests expected the master of the house to rush after Alcibiades and angrily demand his cups back again. The foolish man, however, only said:

"No, let him go. After all, he has only taken half, and if he had liked he might have taken all."

The fact was he was so stupidly fond of Alcibiades that he was ready to give him his richest ornaments. And all the time Alcibiades did not feel respect for these people who were so eager to make his acquaintance. He seemed (at any rate, sometimes) to care much for the company of Socrates. Now, Socrates was an ugly-looking man, who would sit in the market-place of Athens, or in the house of a friend, and talk to the people who gathered about his chair. He was the best and wisest of the citizens, and young men would listen to his speech with great eagerness. I fear, however, that Alcibiades loved many other things quite as much as he loved Socrates, and these things were not always good or useful. He seemed to be a man with many faces. One day he would wear the face of a student, fond of learning. The next day he would wear the face of a clown, taking delight in jokes. He was very changeable.

Having met a well-known and honorable man, Alcibiades went up to him and gave him a box on the ears for no reason whatever, except that he had told his companions he would do so, and they would not believe it. The next morning he called at the house of the old citizen whom he had thus insulted and begged his pardon, and even offered to take any beating which the gentleman might care to give him. But the Athenian bore no ill-will, and freely forgave the daring young man; and I suppose the people passed the story round as a merry jest. He knew the citizens talked about him. He would have been rather miserable if they had not, for he was of a vain and conceited temper. Having bought a very fine dog for a considerable sum of money, he actually cut off the creature's beautiful bushy tail.

"Everybody in the town is talking about the odd way in which you treated your dog," a friend told him.

"This," he replied, "is just what I wanted, for I would rather have the Athenians talk of this action, lest they might find something worse to say about me!"

You will be amused to hear that he, like many Athenians, was fond of breeding a sort of bird called quails. If you look in your book of natural history and examine a picture of a quail, you may not think it a very handsome bird; but it was the fancy of the young men in Athens to make pets of these quails, and Alcibiades used often to carry one under his robe. When he walked in the streets once his quail got loose, and a whole crowd of people went scampering after it to see which should have the honor of restoring it to the owner! They thought Alcibiades a very jolly fellow, and especially when he once sent seven chariots to the Olympic games to take part in the races. Loud were the shouts as he dashed by in one race after another, raising an immense dust about the hoofs of the horses and the wheels of his chariots. He won three prizes, and was so pleased at the result that at his own expense he gave a feast to all the thousands of people who had witnessed the races. When he passed along public places, dressed in a long purple cloak, he was gazed at with much admiration.

"Here is a noble leader for us," some people would say. "See how handsome a man he is; how well he would lead us in war!"

You may remember how I told you of the long, long war (it lasted twenty-eight years) between Athens and Sparta. This struggle was now going on, and the

man in the purple cloak—the man with many faces—
thought he could be a mighty warrior as well as a flute-
player, a quail-breeder, a chariot-racer, and a friend of
Socrates. He would make speeches to the crowds, and
tell them what a great city Athens was, and what victories she would win. One shrewd man, named Timon,
called out to him once:

"Go on, my brave boy, and prosper; for your
prosperity will bring ruin on all this crowd."

He meant that, if the people put their faith in
Alcibiades, it would do no good to the city.

But for a while Alcibiades made himself a
famous name in the wars, and won several battles; and
when the Athenians (as I have related) set sail to conquer Sicily he was captain of one hundred and forty
galleys, fifty-one hundred soldiers in heavy armor, and
thirteen hundred archers and slingers. But he did nothing of much note in Sicily, and was called back to
Athens to answer a charge. It was brought against him
that, one night, in a mad trick, he and his friends had
gone round the streets breaking the images of Hermes
(Her-mees), which stood at the doors of all houses in
Athens. These images were guardians of the homes,
and it was thought a very dreadful thing to interfere
with them. Whether Alcibiades had really done this I
do not know, but people knew his character, and
thought he was quite likely to have insulted the images;
and he was condemned to lose his property, and to be
sent into exile. Where do you think he went to? He
went to Sparta, the city which hated Athens, and was
making war against his own native place. In Sparta he

acted as he did in Athens. He tried to set everybody admiring him. All his fine clothes were hidden away; he was now dressed in coarse garments; his curls were clipped, his hair close-shaven; he ate the Spartan black bread, and drank the black broth, and sat on rough wooden seats, and would have neither carpets nor pictures in his house. This pleased the people of Sparta, and that was all Alcibiades cared for. He pleased them yet more when he joined their armies, and took part in the war against his own countrymen. When, at length, the King of Sparta grew suspicious of him, and thought he was not to be trusted, the man with many faces went over to Asia Minor, and took refuge with a Persian grandee, or nobleman; and the Persians, as you have heard, were bitter foes to the Athenians, but it was all the same to Alcibiades. With the Persians he drank and ate, and sang and hunted; and they also regarded him as a fine fellow. Later on he changed again, and took the side of Athens, and helped in a sea-battle against the Spartans, and won a victory. Other battles were won, and the citizens welcomed him back, gave him his lands again, and crowned him with crowns of gold.

But this glory did not last. The Spartans were masters at the end of the war, and the walls of Athens lay in ruin.

And where was Alcibiades? He had fled to Asia again, and there the Persians slew him, in order to please the powerful Spartans. They had set fire to his house one night. He sallied out, sword in hand, and died fighting.

Certainly, he was clever; and he was witty; and he was handsome; and he was brave; and he was popular—that is, people thought a great deal of him. And do you consider he was good? No. And why not? His aim was always to make the folk admire him, wonder at him, and talk about him. From one thing to another he changed; in one respect only he was forever the same—he never seemed to care for any one but himself. Socrates was ugly; but we honor his memory. Alcibiades was handsome; his cloak was rich purple; his house filled with treasures; but we do not honor his memory. He could not teach even a dog to love him; neither could any man trust him.

IN OLDEN PERSIA

T HE prince and his grandly-dressed nobles walked in procession into the temple, and there a priest stepped forward to meet them.

"Eat this cake of figs," said the priest; and the prince ate the sweetmeat. He was about to become king of the plains and mountains of Persia, and some of his life would be sweet and happy.

"Chew this resin," said the priest; and the prince made a wry face as he ate a piece of turpentine-gum from a pine-tree. Some parts of a king's life are very bitter.

"Drink this sour milk," said the priest; and the prince drank the unpleasant draught. Sweet milk turns sour, and things and people that once were charming may become hateful and disagreeable.

"Put on this old coat," said the priest; and the prince donned a coat which had once been worn by a mighty lord of Persia, named Cyrus. When he wore the coat of the dead lord the new king hoped he would be as great and powerful as Cyrus himself.

A cry rang loudly through the aisles (or passages) of the temple.

"Treason, treason, O king, your life is in danger! In yonder chamber is hiding your brother Cyrus, with intent to kill you."

Guards and nobles rushed to the chamber and dragged out the king's younger brother. Swords were raised to slay him, when the queen-mother flung herself upon the neck of Cyrus (whom she loved better than his brother the king), and twisted the long tresses of her hair about his shoulders; and when he was thus shielded by the queen's hair the soldiers dared not strike. Cyrus was forgiven, but was ordered to proceed to the province of Lydia by the sea, and rule the cities on the coast.

I wish the king had had an easier name for you to read. It was Artaxerxes (*Ar-tags-erk-seez*). He reigned from 405 B.C. to 359 B.C.

Cyrus had his eye on the throne. He meant to be king. To any Greeks who would help him he promised large sums of gold. Before long he had more than twelve thousand Greeks in brazen armor ready to march against his royal brother, and besides these he had one hundred thousand Persians and other folk of Asia.

The king was well liked by many of his people. He had a generous and liberal manner which pleased them. For instance, when he was travelling various gifts were brought to him. One man had nothing to offer, so he ran to a river and filled his hands with water, and held out this very cheap present to the king, who was much pleased, and ordered the man to be rewarded with one thousand darics (a daric was a gold coin).

Prince Cyrus advanced with his army of rebels toward the famous river Euphrates. Across the plain the king had a deep ditch cut, so that an army with horses and baggage could not pass. But the trench or ditch, though it extended for fifty miles, did not quite reach to the river. There was a passage twenty feet wide between the end of the ditch and the river; and the royal army did not think this narrow place was worth guarding. But the army of Cyrus marched that way, and came in face of the immense host led by the king. Then was heard the clash of war. Cyrus, at the head of a troop of horsemen, dashed into the midst of the Persians, killed a nobleman who had aimed a javelin at him, and threw the king from his horse. The king was wounded in the breast, and retreated. Then the rebel prince spurred hotly onward, shouting to the Persians:

"Make way, you slaves, make way."

But a spear pierced his forehead, and he fell from his steed, and soon afterward one of the enemy gave him a death-blow. It was dark when the news came to the king, and he sent thirty men with flaring torches to find the body of Cyrus. Meanwhile, he was glad enough to refresh himself with a drink of muddy water. So thirsty was he that he declared he had never drunk wine that was so delicious; and he gave a heap of treasure to the person who supplied him with the muddy drink. Of course, it is nice and proper to show our gratitude to those who do us a kindness; but it seems to me that the Persian king was intemperate in his gifts. I mean that he gave too much.

Well, you will wonder what became of the Greeks. They would not surrender to the Persians, and marched away, for hundreds of miles, over flat lands, through the mountains, burned by the sun, bitten by the frost, worried by the natives who attacked them by night and day, until at last they came to a certain hill. Those who led the way to the hilltop raised their hands and shouted:

"Thalatta! thalatta! thalatta!"

At this sound the Greeks who lagged behind hurried up, and all cried, as they reached the summit:

"Thalatta! thalatta! thalatta!"

The word "thalatta" is the Greek word for sea; they were looking at the Black Sea, and they knew that along its shores were cities inhabited by Greeks, and they would find friends to help them and ships to carry them back to their wives and children in Greece. This march of the Greeks from Persia to the Black Sea is called the Retreat of the Ten Thousand, and the story of it was written in a book called *The Anabasis*, by one of the captains, named Xenophon (*Zen-o-fon*), who was born about 430 B.C. and died about 357 B.C. Some Greeks were usually to be found at the Persian Court, but I fancy they could never feel quite at home there, for the Greeks were a free people, and the Persians were ready to obey the king in all that he willed. The Persian kings were despots, and their servants bowed to them as if to gods. A certain Greek who was visiting the court was so ashamed of bowing low before the king that he purposely dropped a ring, and stooped to pick it up; and thus he appeared to be bending in a proper manner, and yet he could tell his friends he was merely picking up his ring. What do you think you would have done if you had been in his place?

I have told you how generous the king was in his gifts, and will give you another instance. A Greek friend of his fell ill, and the doctors ordered him plenty of milk; and the king commanded that eighty cows might always be kept for his use, and follow him about if he travelled!

While the king was thus lavish in his gifts to other people, he was willing, when need arose, to live a very hard life himself. He once led an army against some rebel tribes who dwelt in a rugged land, where fogs often made the air dark, and where corn did not grow, and where the folk lived on wild pears, apples, etc. The Persian troops were half-starved; they killed their camels and asses for food, and an ass's head was sold at a very high price. A good example was set by the king. Clad as he was in gold, purple, and shining jewels, he would not shirk the toils of the march. On his back he carried a quiver of arrows, on his arm a buckler, or shield; and, if the army arrived at a rocky path where it was troublesome to climb, he would leap from his horse, and go on foot with hard breathing and heavy labor. And the soldiers stepped out with more spirit when they saw their master share in their hardships. At length they came to a fair place, well set with trees. It was one of the royal parks, kept for the king's pleasure in hunting.

Cold and shivering, the soldiers said to one another:

"If only we might cut down some of those pine-trees or cypress-trees, how we should warm ourselves at the roaring camp-fires."

The king gave order that the timber in the park should be hewn down for firewood. When he saw the men shrink from felling some of the forest trees, he seized an axe, and himself struck the first blow. So the soldiers went to work with a will, and made huge fires, and were happy that night.

In such countries as Persia the life of a king, however worthy he might be, was seldom safe from attack. The king was warned that plotters were coming to put him to death. So he had a door made in the wall of his bedroom, and covered with wall-hangings (or tapestry). In the night, the plotters crept into the royal bedchamber, and advanced with naked swords toward the bed. Then the king rose, slipped behind the tapestry, and through the secret door, and so escaped; and the baffled plotters were caught and punished. The king lived to the age of ninety-four, which was a very remarkable thing for an Eastern despot.

In our own country, as in France, England, Australia, and other countries, the people speak their mind, and meet in open assembly, and elect such men as they will to their Congress or House of Parliament. This is freedom. In Persia there is despotism. We want all the people of the world to be free:

IN OLDEN PERSIA

O sorrowing hearts of slaves,
    We heard you beat from far!
We bring the light that saves;
    We bring the morning star;
And freedom's good we bring you,
    Whence all good things are.

A LAME KING

"WHO is that lame man?"

"The King of Sparta."

"But I thought the Spartans were so proud of their strength, and yet they have a lame king!"

"He is lame, but he is brave: and he is as ready to go to battle as any man with the finest limbs."

The king was Agesilaus (*A-jes-si-lay-us*), who succeeded to the throne 398 B.C., and died about 360 B.C. He spent most of his time in warring with the Persians; so, of course, he had to take his Greeks across the sea in galleys. Once the Persian general proposed to have a talk, or conference, and he fixed a certain place and hour for meeting the Spartan king. The place was a grove of trees in a meadow; and Agesilaus, arriving there first with some of his friends, sat down on the long grass in the shade. Simple as the couch was, it was fair and easy enough for Spartans. When the Persian general reached the spot, his slaves laid soft rugs and cushions on the ground for their master to sit on during the conversation. But when he caught sight of the Spartans on the grass, the general felt ashamed to appear so fond of delicate cushions, and he also seated himself on the ground.

Enemies closer to Sparta than the Persians were now threatening, and Agesilaus recrossed the sea, and led his soldiers back to his native land, through rocky passes, across mountain streams, and past many a foeman's town. He had tried to stretch his empire far and wide, instead of staying in his own country and resting content with the kingdom he was born in. At length he fought his way back to the city of Sparta, and once more dwelt in his humble palace. Plain was his house, plain his furniture, and plain the dress of his daughters. The very doors told how little the Spartan kings cared for show, for the doors at the entrance of the royal abode were said to be about seven hundred years old.

The king had no love for display and glitter, either in houses or people. He was asked to go and hear a clever fellow who could whistle so exactly like a nightingale that you could fancy you heard the lovely bird singing in the forest. The king, however, said, "Thank you, no; I prefer to hear the nightingale itself."

Again, there was a doctor who was very vain of a name which the people gave him. They called him Jupiter, because he had (so they said) cured quite a number of folk of their ailments. You know that Jupiter was the master of all the gods. One day the foolish man was writing a letter to King Agesilaus, and he began thus: "Doctor Jupiter wishes the king health." To this the monarch replied: "King Agesilaus wishes Doctor Jupiter more common sense!"

In his manners in the house he was very homely, and he often played with his children. A nobleman, calling to see him, opened the door of the royal nursery, and stood still in astonishment when he beheld the mighty lord of Sparta galloping round with a walking-stick between his legs for a horse!

"Are you a father?" asked Agesilaus.

"No, sir."

"Well, wait till you are, and have children of your own, and then you will understand."

In the wars that followed between Sparta and other Greek States, Agesilaus was helped by some of his neighbors; but they complained of having more than their fair share of the fighting. This was said at a big meeting of the Spartans and their allies (friends). So the king asked them all to sit down, and then he bade his crier or herald summon the men of any trade to stand up:

"Potters, arise!"

And they arose up.

"Braziers, arise!"

And they arose up.

"Carpenters, arise!"

And they arose up; and then the masons, and so on. But not a single Spartan stood; for the Spartans did no hand-work, but left such labor to their slaves, or helots.

Then the king smiled, and said:

"You see, my people do nothing but fight, while you others work at various crafts, and therefore I think Sparta takes its fair share of war."

Yes, that was right, as an answer to the persons who complained. But I think it was a pity that so fine a nation as the Spartans should have no industry but the art of war. Potters, braziers, carpenters, masons, etc.—the more we have of these, and the fewer soldiers, the better.

So proud were the Spartans of their skill and courage in battle that they even despised the man who brought news of a defeat. Indeed, such news seldom arrived. Those who fled away from the enemy were called "tremblers," and the tremblers had to wear coats of patchwork colors, and to shave only one half of their beards!

A fierce battle took place with the Thebans, and the Spartans were beaten. Just as the news came to the city the people were engaged in sports, racing, and wrestling in the open-air theatre. The magistrates who sat in the theatre would not allow the games to stop. Each race was run; each exercise was finished, as if there was nothing to do but make merry. Next day, after the names of the men slain in the battle had been learned, all who had lost any sons, brothers, or friends went about the streets looking gay and cheerful; and those who had lost no friends shut themselves in their houses as if in mourning. You see, the Spartans were proud to give their sons to the service of their fatherland, and thought it quite an honor for a man to be killed in the wars. But so many "tremblers" had fled from the battle I have spoken of that the magistrates did not dare to dress them in the patchwork coats. Ere long the enemy appeared before the walls of Sparta, and set fire to houses outside the city. It is said that no foe had trodden the soil of Sparta for six hundred years. The women looked from the walls, and saw with terror the smoke that rose from the burning villages outside. Agesilaus was most cautious. He kept his men inside the walls, and would not be tempted into sallying forth; and at last the Thebans withdrew. At one moment the king was threatened with a danger in his own fortress. A party of two hundred of his own followers gathered at a temple, as if to begin a rebellion. What was to be done? Was Agesilaus to fight his own citizens? He used his wits, and thought of a plan. Advancing with only one attendant to the gate of the temple, he called out:

"You have made a mistake. I did not order you all to assemble here. Some of you are to march to that position" (pointing to a certain place on his right), "and others there" (pointing to a place on his left), "and others yonder."

So quiet and firm was his manner that they obeyed, and so the force was broken up. He took care, however, to arrest fifteen of the ringleaders, and they were put to death the next night. After a while the Thebans made an assault upon the town, but were hurled back, and they retreated, and, their captain being slain in a fresh battle, a peace was concluded.

Even when Agesilaus grew old—even more than eighty years old—he still took a joy in war; and, at the request of a prince of Egypt, he sailed to that country with an army, and prepared to fight the prince's enemies. This he did for pay, and not because he cared which side was in the right. A vast crowd of Egyptians waited on the shore for the coming of the Spartan fleet. Agesilaus landed, and sat down on some grass. When the Egyptians beheld the little lame old king, they could scarcely believe this man was the famous leader of whose exploits (deeds) they had heard so many stirring tales. They offered him presents of rich food. He took the solid part of it, such as the veal and geese, but would not taste the pastry and sweetmeats.

"You can take those things to my helots" (slaves), he said.

I am rather ashamed to tell you that, after all, he did not assist the prince who had invited him across the seas; but he went over to the enemy, and the war soon ended. But a new peril happened. A host of rebels appeared, and marched toward the city occupied by Agesilaus and his Egyptian allies. They dug a ditch, or trench, nearly all round. Agesilaus watched their work, but did not interfere till the trench was almost a circle. Then he sallied forth and attacked, marching straight onward; he had no need to guard the flanks or sides of his army, for the very ditch which the rebels had dug protected him from their onrush. And thus he easily won a victory.

At the close of the war he took away much money, and sailed for Sparta. But a wintry storm drove his vessels back to the African coast, and the old king, worn out with many hardships, died in a harbor of a strange land. His body was embalmed, or covered with wax, and carried to Sparta.

We cannot help admiring the boldness and sturdiness of the Spartans; but, for all that, we have to remember that they have given us no books, no poems, no pictures, and no beautiful buildings such as the Greeks of Athens produced. They loved only the glory of war.

A MARTYR KING

"THAT young man's cloak is a very plain one, and yet he walks along the street with a step that is stately, as if he were not a common person. Who is he?"

"He is the king."

"Why does he wear so plain a dress? Why does he not show gay colors and adorn his body with gold, as other kings do?"

"I believe he wants us all to live in a simple way, like our fathers in olden times."

So spake two citizens of Sparta.

Yes, that was the aim of King Agis (A-jis). He reigned 244–240 B.C. As I have often told you, the Spartan folk had once clothed themselves in the roughest garb, lain on hard beds, eaten coarse food, and spent much of their time in exercise in sport or war. But now the ancient ways had almost died out. A few people were very rich, and possessed most of the land; and the great bulk of the people were poor, ragged, ill-fed, and in debt. When the young king saw the misery of Sparta, he thought of the days of old, and he longed to bring about a change or reform. One day he sat talking with his mother and grandmother.

"You are both rich," he said to them, "and if you will do as I ask you will set a noble example to other rich persons, and they will follow it."

"What is that?"

"I want you to give up a large share of your estates, and I will do the same; and if many of the richer class do likewise there will be an immense amount of land to spare for a purpose which I have set my heart on. I will divide it into small allotments for the people, so that each Spartan may then be a landholder, and have soil on which to grow corn and fruit for himself and his family. The unemployed will then have work to do, and the folk who are now idle and careless will become industrious and sober."

The royal ladies listened eagerly, and their hearts were warmed with the same desire as filled the young king's heart. They called a meeting of other Spartan ladies, and said to them:

"We shall give up much of our wealth for the good of the people. Ask your husbands to do as we do, and our ancient nation will have peace and contentment once more."

When the news of the king's plan spread among the poor folk there was much joy; but among the rich there was anger, for they thought they should now lose land, money, and comfort. The Spartans had the custom of choosing two kings instead of only one. Agis was the younger king; the elder was Leonidas, and

Leonidas took the side of the wealthy class; and thus the country was divided. For a time the party of Agis gained the upper hand. Leonidas fled away, and his son-in-law, a prince, was made king in his place. As the son-in-law had a troublesome Greek name, I will simply call him the prince.

One day a vast crowd of Spartans had come together in the market-place to see the burning of the bonds. A bond is a paper which is held for a debt. If you owed me a sum of money, and you had agreed by putting your name on a certain paper to repay me the money, the paper would be called a bond; and if I destroyed the bond I should do away with the debt, and you would no longer be bound to pay. The king had ordered all persons who held bonds to bring them to the bonfire that was lit in the market-place. The bonds were cast into the flames, and the people shouted with gladness as they saw the papers crackle and smoke. But the money-lenders and bondholders walked away with sorrow in their faces and bitter feelings in their hearts. King Agis had given up for the people's use his ploughed land and his cattle pastures, as well as an immense sum of money. His mother and grandmother and some of their friends had also yielded up their possessions. But most of the rich folk were still waiting. They had no will to strip themselves of their goods.

It happened that a war was taking place in another part of Greece, and King Agis had promised to help one side with his troops. So he led an army of young Spartans to the field of war. On the march he was most strict in forbidding his warriors to hurt any man or any person's property in the villages they passed through. While he was thus absent, however, the rich class had made rebellion, and brought back Leonidas to the throne. This was done before Agis had time to return and prevent it. It was the hour of danger to the prince and to his friend Agis. Each of them fled to a different temple. Bands of enemies surrounded the buildings and watched. No Greek might be slain inside a holy temple, but if he issued forth then his life might be taken.

First, I will tell you what happened to the prince. His wife heard of his peril, and she took her two children and hurried to the temple and sat beside her husband. The guards told Leonidas, and he came and saw his daughter; her hair was fallen on her shoulders, and her dress was the dress of a mourning woman.

"Father," she cried, "when you went into exile I followed you, and tried to console you in your trouble. But now it is my husband who suffers. So I am bound to be wretched, first as a daughter and then as a wife. But I declare to you I will not see my husband die, for I will slay myself before you can touch him."

Having said this, the lady rested her head on her husband's shoulder, while the little children wept for their father's sake. And Leonidas was much moved, and he whispered with his friends, and then he gave command to the prince to go right out of Sparta, taking his wife and children with him. So the lady gave one child to her husband and carried one herself, and they four passed out into exile.

Next I will tell you of the end of Agis. For a while the king, Leonidas, had sent fair messages to him, and told him he hoped he would come out and take his part again in the governing of the country. Agis put little trust in these fine words; but he did at least believe Leonidas when the elder king said he might safely leave the temple each day to go to the bath at the end of the street. Several times Agis had visited the bath and returned to the temple unhurt, and so he came to think all was well. Three of his friends would meet him on the road and talk words of good cheer. But they had treason in their souls. In order to gain the favor of Leonidas, they had prepared a plot for the capture of the young king.

One evening, as the sky was getting dusky, they met Agis as usual walking from the bath, and they chatted with him until they reached the corner of a street that led to the prison. Suddenly one of them flung a cloak over the king's head, while the others held his arms. Other persons rushed up, and the party dragged Agis to the jail. The strong gates opened and soon closed again. A number of soldiers were posted about the building lest the citizens should seek to release the imprisoned king.

Before long, five magistrates sat in a chamber of the jail. By the light of lamps they tried the royal captive. The trial was very short. The questions they asked were few. The last question was this:

"Do you not repent of what you have done in Sparta?"

"No, indeed," answered the heroic king. "I shall never repent of so glorious a plan, even though I see death before my eyes."

The five judges gave sentence that Agis should die. The officers carried him into a small room, from which he should never come out alive. Meanwhile, crowds of people had come to the prison, and were waving lanterns and torches in the darkness outside, wanting to know what was being done with the king. Alas! Agis lay dead. He had been strangled. Just before he died he saw one of the officers weeping.

"My friend," he said, "weep not for me. I have done no evil, and I am happier than those men who treat me unjustly."

The gates were opened for a moment to let in the king's mother and grandmother. The ladies hastened in, hoping to be in time to save their dear one's life. First of all the old grandmother was allowed to go into the inner chamber.

Then the mother. But when she entered she beheld her son's dead body, and she also beheld the dead body of her aged mother. When she saw this she knelt and kissed Agis, and said:

"My son, you were too honest and too generous a king for this country."

"If you approve your son's conduct," cried one of the three traitors who had seized the king on his way from the bath, "you shall share his reward."

"May all this be for the good of Sparta," sighed the queen.

THE·DOOM·OF·AGIS·KING·OF·SPARTA·

Presently she herself was slain, and the three bodies were carried from the prison in the sight of the people, and the people were struck with terror, and they went to their homes.

Agis had died while trying to reform the condition of Sparta. He sought the good of his country, and he was put to death. Therefore we call him a martyr. He died in the year 240 B.C., more than two thousand years ago. Yet, you see, the world has not forgotten the young king and the Spartan ladies, and their noble purpose of helping their native land. They pointed to a goal for the people to go to, though they never lived to reach the happier place themselves. As we remember Agis and the brave women, we seem to see a light shine about us—the light of their good deeds:

> Say not they die, those martyr souls
>   Whose life is winged with purpose fine;
> Who leave us, pointing to the goals,
>   Who learn to conquer and resign.
>
> Such cannot die; they vanquish time,
>   And fill the world with growing light,
> Making the human life sublime
>   With memories of their sacred might.
>   (*Malcolm Quin.*)

A VALIANT HELPER

"YOU don't look after yourself enough. You are not doing your duty."

"Why do you say so? I take care of my wife and children, and I serve my fatherland."

"Yes, but you do not get all the money you can."

"Money? Oh, well, I can do without much money. Yonder man needs money. He is both lame and blind."

The person who thus spoke lightly of money was a famous soldier, Pelopidas (*Pel-op-id-as*), who lived in the Greek city of Thebes (*Theebz*). Strong was he in body, and he loved to try his strength with others in the wrestling-ring, and in hunting boars and deer in the forests. Noble was he in soul, for he was ever ready to go to the help of people who were ill-used or in any kind of distress.

In the year 379 B.C. a band of Spartans suddenly marched into the city and made themselves masters of the castle. This they did by the wish of certain noblemen, who hoped to rule the city themselves, under the power of the Spartans. Pelopidas was then quite a young man. He and a number of his friends were obliged to fly from Thebes, for they were on the side of the people, and the unjust noblemen sought to take their lives. The heart of Pelopidas burned with a desire to set his city free, and often he said to his companions in exile:

"We ought not to rest here while our beloved land is in the hands of evil rulers. It would be glorious to win back freedom for Thebes. Will you not join with me in saving our native city?"

They said they would. First they sent a secret message to a citizen named Charon (*Kar-on*), who promised to take them into his house in Thebes, and there they would prepare for an attack on the tyrants. A band of young Thebans set out for the city. But as it would not be wise for so large a body to show themselves at once, twelve of them went on in front dressed in the plain garments of country folk, and taking with them dogs and hunting-poles as if they were engaged in the chase. Their comrade, Charon, was expecting them. But one of the Thebans, who knew of the plot, felt afraid, and bade a particular friend ride quickly to the young men and warn them not to come any farther, for the peril was too great. This messenger hurried home to saddle a horse. He could not find the bridle.

"Hi! hi!" he cried to his wife. "Where is the bridle? Fetch it instantly."

"I don't know where your bridle is," she replied.

"You ought to know! I am waiting for it, and I must be off at once. Where is it, I say?"

The woman answered him angrily, and he shouted rudely in return. Then out came her sisters and serving-maids, and they all screamed in chorus:

"You bad man, you! How dare you talk so rudely to your wife, and all about a stupid bridle!"

Thus the time passed, and the message was never taken.

Meanwhile, the twelve hunters (one of whom was Pelopidas) had entered the town without being specially noticed, for there had been a fall of snow, and most folk were glad to stay indoors. And before long the hunters and their comrades were assembled in Charon's dwelling, forty-eight in all. In the evening they had put on their breast-plates, and buckled their swords to their sides, when a loud knocking was heard at Charon's door.

"Who is there?"

"The rulers of Thebes have sent me," said a voice, "to command you, O Charon, to attend before them immediately."

At once they supposed the plot was found out. Some of the young men looked in doubt at Charon. Could they trust him? Would he betray them? When Charon read their thoughts by the expression of their faces, he took his little son, and gave the child to Pelopidas.

"Here," he said, "is my son, and, if you find I am a traitor, you may slay my child."

Some of them shed tears, and cried:

"No, no! Put your son in a place of safety, lest the tyrants kill both him and you."

"I could not," he answered, "wish any better fate for my boy than to die with his father and so many friends for the sake of Thebes."

Now, a letter had been brought all the way from Athens to the leader of the tyrants, to warn him of the doings of Pelopidas. But the chief tyrant was deep in his wine, and the enjoyment of feast and music, and, on receiving the letter, he would not read it, but said:

"Business to-morrow!"

Ah, business to-morrow! So he put off till the morrow what might have been done that day, and when Charon came he had no clear questions to ask him. All he could say was that a rumor had reached him that certain plotters had come to Charon's house. When Charon replied that it was not wise to believe every tale that went about the city, the tyrant let him go. Presently a noise was heard at the gates, a noise of laughing and singing, and a crowd of people rushed in clad in women's gowns, and with thick wreaths of pine and poplar leaves about their heads. The company at the tables clapped their hands, expecting sport. But the pretended women cast aside their gowns, and fell upon the guests with deadly weapons, and the banquet was turned into mourning and bloodshed. And people ran wildly through the streets, carrying torches in the dark, and wondering what had come to pass.

In the castle fifteen hundred Spartans stood to arms, but dared not issue forth; and next day, being surrounded by the Thebans, they agreed to yield up the fortress if they were allowed to march home to Sparta. And this being promised, the Spartans left the city, and all the citizens gave honor to the valiant Pelopidas and his friends who had restored liberty to Thebes. Thereafter Pelopidas led many an assault on Spartan cities and Spartan troops, and the tribes round about, who had lived in fear of the Spartan warriors, now looked to Pelopidas as their helper and savior.

Among these tribes were the Thessalians, who lived in dread of a tyrant named Alexander. This brutal prince would bury alive men that had offended him; or he would clothe them in the skins of bears and wild boars and set dogs to worry them to death. The Thessalians begged the brave Pelopidas to go to their help. Then, swift and dauntless, went forth the Theban captain with a band of warriors, and when he appeared the tyrant was smit with terror, and made no resistance, but bowed humbly and said he would do the bidding of Pelopidas. But, not long afterward, Alexander sought again to oppress the people, and Pelopidas, almost alone, went to warn the tyrant to cease his evil conduct. Seeing him unguarded, Alexander caused the noble Theban to be arrested and flung into a prison. Yet he did not dare to slay him. As Pelopidas sat in his cell one day a lady entered, and gazed at his pale face and his disordered hair. In a kind tone she said:

"I pity your wife."

"And who are you that pity my wife?"

"The queen."

"I pity the queen," said he, "for being the wife of a cruel tyrant."

And soon he found that she was ashamed of her husband's evil deeds, and longed to see the end of his wickedness.

The friends of Pelopidas came to his rescue, and at the approach of their army Alexander gave up his prisoner and craved for peace.

At that time the Greek States were sending ambassadors to the King of Persia, and Pelopidas was chosen to go in the name of the city of Thebes. The King of Persia took more pleasure in meeting the valiant Theban than any of the others. To the ambassadors he usually gave gifts. For instance, to one—an Athenian—he gave gold and silver, a grand bed and servants to make it, eighty cows and herdsmen to tend them, and a litter or travelling-chair to carry him about! But when the Persian king asked Pelopidas what gift he desired, the reply was:

"I desire that you will treat all the Greeks as free and independent."

Thus Pelopidas sought the good of the people, and not presents for himself.

In the year 364 B.C. a message again came from the Thessalians asking for help against Alexander. Pelopidas was about to march when darkness fell on the earth during an eclipse of the sun. He would not delay for that, but hurried on to meet the foe. Alexander awaited him in a valley at the base of some steep hills.

Theban horsemen drove the enemy back. Then Alexander's men tried to mount the heights; the Thebans followed; among the rocks and cliffs the warriors scrambled and fought. When Pelopidas caught sight of the tyrant he rushed in front of his troops to attack Alexander. A shower of javelins flew through the air, and Pelopidas fell dead. After his men had gained the victory, the Thessalians came and asked for the honor of burying their noble friend. Soldiers and citizens gathered about the dead chief, and mourned with heavy hearts. The people cut off their own hair and the manes of the war-horses in token of their sorrow for the generous Theban who would nevermore aid the oppressed.

And now for the end of Alexander. One night he slept in his royal bed, guarded by a fierce dog, who would fly at anybody except his master and mistress and the slave that fed him. The queen told the slave to take the dog away. Then she covered the stairs with wool to soften the sound of footsteps. Taking her husband's sword from his pillow, she showed it to her three brothers, and then bade them ascend. They climbed the stairs, and then they paused in fear. The queen, holding a lamp, sternly ordered them to enter. And they went in and slew him. Ah, yes! it is sad that death should have to be dealt out to evil-doers. But cruelty is a hateful thing, and justice is a glorious thing, and the poor and needy must be delivered.

DION

"YOUR beard is growing again, sir. Will you have it shaved?"

"No, certainly not. Bring the red-hot coal, as before."

"Yes, sir."

The servant fetched a live coal, and singed the hair of the king's chin. The king was afraid lest his foes might tempt the barber to kill him with the razor; therefore, he would not allow a razor to be used. Very few persons loved this king, whose name was Dionysius (*Dy-on-y-si-us*) the Elder, born 430 B.C., died 367 B.C. Once he had been a clerk. Step by step he had climbed to power, and now he dwelt in a royal house, overlooking the blue waters of the harbor of Syracuse (*Sy-ra-kuze*) in the island of Sicily. Men who thus obtained power without the wish of the people were known by the Greeks as tyrants.

"Your brother is at the gate, sir, and desires to see you," said the attendant.

"Strip off his clothes," replied the king. The visitor's clothes were stripped off by the guards, and searched for daggers or other weapons which might have been used to injure the king; and a new suit was then given to the prince, and he was allowed to enter the royal chamber. You see that the tyrant was very suspicious.

One day a brother of the king was talking to him about the plan of a certain place, and he thought he would trace it on the floor of the room, just as you might draw a plan of a house with pencil on paper.

"Lend me your spear," said the king's brother to a soldier who stood by. He then marked out some lines on the floor. But the tyrant sat fidgeting in terror lest the spear should be aimed at his own heart. When his brother had left he caused the soldier to be put to death.

Sometimes, instead of slaying the persons he hated, he ordered them to be taken below. The prisoners were led down some dark stairs, through many narrow passages cut out of the solid rock, and then locked up in cells, where no sunlight gleamed, and no sound of the voices of earth was heard.

The tyrant had two wives; and the brother of one of them was Dion, a wise and brave man, who did his best to check the evil deeds of the king. Often would he speak to him, and seek to turn his heart to kinder ways. At last he said to the king:

"There is a learned man in Athens by whom I have been taught many useful lessons, and I believe it would interest you to hear him. Shall I send for him to come and see you? He is a philosopher of whom all the world has heard. I mean Plato" (*Play-to*).

"Send for him, if you will," answered the king.

Plato agreed to visit the city of Syracuse, and made the voyage in a galley across the Mediterranean Sea. The king received him in his marble palace, and Plato lectured to a richly-dressed company. He spoke of the manner in which men should labor, whether kings or working folk. And at the end of his lecture he said:

"Thus we see, O king, that they who act justly have peace in their hearts, but they who act unjustly are unhappy."

"Good! quite true," cried some of the audience (that is, the people listening).

"I do not admire your teaching," said the king. "What is the use of such talk? Why did you come to Sicily?"

"To find an honest man," replied Plato.

"I suppose you think you have come for nothing, then?" sneered the king.

Not long afterward word was sent to Plato that the tyrant no longer desired his presence on the island, and that it would be well for him to return to Athens. A ship's captain—a Spartan sailor—approached Plato, and said he had the royal orders to carry the philosopher back to Greece; and Plato embarked in the Spartan vessel. The king had secretly bidden the captain to sell Plato for a slave. "For," said he, "it must be all the same to him whether he is a free man or a slave, since he told me that the just man, whether free or slave, is always happy."

At a seaport in Greece Plato was sold in the market-place for one hundred dollars. However, a friend of his happened to be there at the time, bought him again, and sent him in safety to Athens. So Dion's plan to change his royal master's character came to naught. In the year 367 B.C. the tyrant lay ill, and asked his physicians for a sleeping-draught—that is, a medicine which would soothe his nerves and send him to sleep. They gave him a very strong dose. He drank it, and never woke again.

The king's son, Dionysius the younger, came to the throne. When a youth he had been kept very much at home by his father, who feared lest he should become a favorite with the people and try to gain the crown. The young prince amused himself at carpentry, and made little chariots, candle-sticks, chairs, and tables. On the death of the old king the prince's friends filled the palace with the noise of their feasts and music. For ninety days the revel went on. Wine was freely drunk from morning to night, and tipsy courtiers, crowned with roses, staggered along the lovely marble pavements of the royal house. Now and then a quiet, grave man looked on at the rowdy scene, and went away with a sigh. It was Dion.

Dion again thought of Plato, and, finding the young king in a sober humor, he persuaded him to invite the wise man of Athens to the Sicilian island once more. Again Plato came, and he was borne from the harbor to the palace in the king's own chariot. In conversation with the king Plato tried to lift up his thoughts to nobler things than wine and dainty eating and low-minded companions. The king and some of his friends resolved to change their lives. They would now study science, they would learn geometry (or the science of measurement), and con the lessons of Euclid, such as boys still con at school and college. So eager were the young men in their new study that groups of them were to be seen in various rooms of the palace holding sticks in their hands, and scratching the figures of Euclid in the dust which was spread on the marble floors. Wherever you went you would see squares, circles, and triangles; and you would hear the young nobles cry, "This line is parallel to that," or, "This angle is equal to those two angles," and so on.

The fancy for schooling and learning did not last long. Dion became hateful in the sight of the king, and was banished from the land of Sicily. Plato stayed on for a while, but the king regarded him less and less, and, at length, hinted that it was time for him to depart. Just before Plato left he was sitting at a banquet with Dionysius, and the king said:

"I suppose, Plato, when you return to Athens, you will pick my character to pieces before your friends, and tell them all my faults."

"I hope, sir," was Plato's reply, "that we shall have enough to talk about without talking of you!"

Soon afterward he sailed for Greece. Meanwhile Dion brooded over the troubles of his country, and longed to be able to set aside the tyrant, and give a free government to the citizens of Syracuse. He told his thoughts to his friends who had also been banished. Eight hundred of them assembled on a Grecian island,

and prepared to travel to Sicily and deliver their country from the oppressor.

It was now midsummer, and the moon was at
the full, and the eastern wind was blowing, day by day,
and they would need this wind to carry them quickly
across the sea. The eight hundred patriots—lovers of
their fatherland—put on their bright armor, and
marched to the temple of Apollo, and asked the God
of the sun to bless them in their great adventure. The
next night the moon was eclipsed, and the warriors
were uneasy at the black shadow. One of Dion's
friends explained the meaning of this sign, or omen.
The bright moon, he said, was the tyrant of Syracuse,
and Dion was the black shadow which would creep
over the tyrant's glory and hide it! And when they
heard that, in Syracuse, some little pigs had been born
without ears, Dion's friends declared that the dwellers
in that city would no longer have any ears for the
commands or laws of the tyrant!

Dion's fleet made for the open sea. The vessels
carried, besides the weapons of the eight hundred,
piles of shields, javelins, and darts for the use of new
recruits who would join at the landing of the army.
The cliffs of Sicily came in sight. Then arose a violent
storm of thunder and lightning, the north wind blew
the ships toward Africa, and a pelting rain drenched
the patriots to the skin. At one point the fleet nearly
perished on rocks, at another it only just escaped running upon a huge sand-bank. Calmer weather followed, and, under a fair sky, Dion's ships again
appeared off the coast of the Sicilian isle. The eight

hundred landed, and Dion told them they might now take a rest after the hardships of the voyage.

"No, no!" they cried; "lead us at once to Syracuse."

Dion took them at their word. They put aside all luggage which was not immediately wanted, and they began the march in high spirits. Before long crowds of Sicilians had flocked to Dion's support, and he had five thousand men.

"Liberty, liberty!" they shouted as they marched.

"Liberty, liberty!" was the cry when they saw the tall towers of Syracuse, and the strong citadel (a fortress), and the ships in the harbor.

The joyful citizens came forth from the gates, clothed in white, and gave a loud welcome to the army of Dion.

Dion, dressed in splendid armor, entered the city of Syracuse; a friend on each side wore a garland of flowers; a hundred foreign soldiers followed as his body-guard, and the rest of the army marched joyously behind. The citizens raised loud shouts of "Liberty!" They had suffered the hard rule of the tyrants for forty-eight years.

At the sound of a trumpet silence was made, and a herald cried to the people, and said Syracuse would now enjoy a free government. Then Dion climbed to the top of the Tower of the Sundial—a sundial, as you know, being a slab of wood or stone, with a piece projecting (or sticking out) and throwing a shadow by which to tell the time. The multitude stood below and listened while he begged them to stand firm when the tyrant Dionysius returned from Italy, and when the tyrant's soldiers sallied out from the citadel. This citadel was a strong-walled fortress in the town, and it was guarded by men who were in the pay of the bad king.

Round the citadel Dion built a fence, from behind which his people could shoot arrows and stones at the garrison. Suddenly the garrison sallied out. Many of the citizens fled. Dion was in the thick of the fray, and his head was gashed by a lance. Then he retired from the battle, but rode about the streets, though his head was bleeding, and besought all the men to hurry to the aid of those who were fighting. Many of the enemy lay dead; and, next day, the people of Syracuse crowned Dion with a crown of gold.

Yet Dion was not the only leader. A fleet of galleys lay in the harbor, and it was under the command of a bold admiral, whom many of the citizens liked better than Dion. The admiral tried to gain the love of the folk by fair words and promises. He even said that all the lands ought to be equally divided, and many of the poorer men were pleased at the idea, and resolved to support the admiral rather than Dion. Meanwhile the King Dionysius had come back from Italy, stayed awhile in the citadel, and then, fearing lest the fort should be captured, he stole secretly away with his treasures, and returned no more.

The folk met together to choose twenty-five men for the city council. While they were preparing for the election, a most dreadful thunderstorm had broken over the town, and scarce any one dared stir out-of-doors. When at last the people assembled, a new fright seized them. An ox, which had been standing quietly in the highway, broke loose, and ran madly through the crowd; and the citizens counted this a bad omen—that is, a sign of evil things about to happen. They did not choose Dion for the council, but they chose the admiral. Dion saw that trouble was overshadowing Syracuse, and he and his faithful followers began to leave the city. Some of the Syracusans attacked him. Dion had no heart to fight his own countrymen. Pointing to the dark citadel, on the ramparts of which the foes of liberty were watching, he said:

"Yonder are our enemies. Do you wish them to see us at war with each other?"

The mob would not listen. Then Dion bade his warriors advance with a clash of weapons and stern faces, but not to strike; and the people fled, and even the women, looking from the windows, laughed at their sudden flight. Dion and his troops encamped some way out of the city, and ill did it fare with Syracuse after his going. The tyrant sent a fleet of ships, filled with provisions, to the help of the garrison of the fort. Four of these ships were taken by the citizens, and, in their joy, the people made high festival, and sang songs of victory, and rolled drunken in the streets. The captain of the tyrant's fleet saw the disorder of the city, landed his soldiers, killed many of the men, and dragged a crowd of shrieking children and women to the gates of the citadel and made them captives. Then the Syracusans met in great grief, and looked at one another in silence and in despair. Presently a voice cried:

"Send for Dion!"

Ah, send for Dion! They had ill-used the patriot leader, and now they longed for his strong arm to fight the foe, and once more give liberty to Syracuse. Seven men were sent to Dion's camp. It was sunset as they reached the spot, and by the light of the camp-fires the unhappy messengers told Dion and his friends what a plight the city was in. Dion arose to reply, but at first the tears rolled down his cheeks and he could not utter a word. Then at last he said:

"Comrades, I cannot hesitate. My beloved city is perishing. If I cannot save it, I will at least hasten thither and fall beneath the ruins of my country."

The whole army shouted that they were ready to march.

"Go to your tents," said the commander, "and refresh yourselves, and then meet again, each warrior with his armor, for this very night we shall go to Syracuse."

Before Dion reached the city the tyrant's garrison had again broken out. More citizens were slain in the streets; more houses were aflame. When the news came to Dion he and his men no longer marched— they ran through the streets amid the smoke of the burning dwellings. Oh, then were heard the glad cries of citizens welcoming the deliverer, and they rejoiced to see once again the man whom they had driven from their midst! The enemy hastened to retreat into the citadel, and Dion was again master of Syracuse.

"Now," said some of his friends—"now is the time to punish the evil men who rebelled against your rule."

"Not so," replied Dion; "it is not enough to be kind to men of virtue—we should forgive those who work us injury."

Ere long the broken fence round the citadel was repaired, and the place was besieged. The garrison were being starved out. Their captain offered to surrender if he and part of the defenders might sail away in five galleys. This request was granted, and one day all the citizens assembled on the shores of the harbor and watched the five galleys pass out and leave the fair island of Sicily in peace. Syracuse was free.

I wish I could close the story here. But I must tell dark incidents as well as bright. The admiral was still jealous of Dion's power, and still drew a portion of the people away from their obedience to the government of the man who had saved the city. One day a band of men broke into the admiral's house and slew him. It is said that Dion knew of their purpose, and allowed it. He certainly felt uneasy in his mind about the deed. His conscience told him he might have prevented it, and did not. When he walked outside his mansion one evening his mind was disturbed, and he fancied he saw a terrible Fury coming toward him with a broom in her hand. The Greeks used to think of the Furies as three awful giantesses whose bodies were black, whose eyes dripped drops of blood, and in whose hair were snakes entwined; and they flew on great wings, and bore daggers or whips in their hands to punish evil-doers. This story reminds us of Shakespeare's tale of Macbeth, the Scottish nobleman who murdered the king and other men, and then could not sleep for fear of their ghosts.

And perhaps some of the citizens feared that Dion would now in turn become a tyrant. A number of men resolved to take his life. They broke into his house, and Dion fell by the stroke of a short sword 354 B.C. Yet the memory of the patriot who had done and suffered so much for Syracuse was dear to thousands of the people. The leader of the plot by which he lost his life was unable to stay in Syracuse, nor would any city in the whole island receive him. At length he was killed by two of his companions. And the story went round among the Sicilian folk that he was slain by the very same short sword which had caused the death of the noble Dion.

THE MAN WHO SAVED SICILY

T HE beautiful island of Sicily had been so wasted
by war and burning in the third century B.C. that
the orchards and vineyards yielded little fruit, the
towns were dull, and the trading-ships no longer
passed in large numbers round the coast. Then came
men from Carthage in Africa, and they landed on the
island, thinking to take possession. These Punic warriors (as the men of Carthage were called) were so
strong and cunning that the people of Sicily were in
great fear, and sent messengers to the seaside town of
Corinth, in Greece, to ask for help; for the Greeks in
Sicily had first come from Corinth. The citizens of
Corinth chose a man named Timoleon (*Tim-o´-le-on*) to
go to the help of Sicily.

By night Timoleon set sail with ten ships. The
wind blew fair toward the west; on a sudden the heav-
ens seemed torn in two, and a flame leaped down and
lit up the vessel in which Timoleon rode, and all his
followers were much cheered at this happy sign. At
least, so the story goes; but you need not believe all the
marvels in old histories. You would think all the Sicilians would welcome the saviors from Greece; but it
was not so, and a party of them barred the road by
which Timoleon, after landing on the island, was

marching to Syracuse, the capital. Near the place of battle stood a temple to the God of War, guarded by a hundred dogs. I dare say you have heard speak of "letting loose the dogs of war," for the dog was thought to be an animal beloved by the Battle-god. Timoleon put the foe to flight, he himself heading the Corinthians, and running forward with his buckler on his arm. To him, as he approached the temple after the victory, came many people, who declared that during the fight the doors of the holy building had opened of themselves, and the spear in the hand of the god's statue shook, and the face of the god dripped with sweat.

Not long afterward the Corinthians pressed their way into the city of Syracuse and made themselves masters of the strong-walled fortress or citadel. Timoleon, however, stayed in camp some distance away.

Two men were sent to put him to death. These assassins had daggers under their coats, and mingled with the crowd of people who filled the approach to the temple, waiting to see Timoleon come to offer sacrifice to the War-god. They edged themselves nearer and nearer. They were ready to strike. One of them suddenly fell to the ground. He had been killed by a blow from behind, and the man who struck him fled for his life through the crowd, and up to the top of a high rock. The other assassin in much fear ran to the altar, held on to it, and shrieked out to Timoleon:

"Sir, have mercy on me, in the name of this holy altar!"

The man on the top of the rock was fetched down.

"Why did you slay yonder Sicilian?" he was asked.

"Because," he replied, "this Sicilian slew my father; and there are people here who know what I say is true."

Yes, it was true. Strange, indeed, that he should have chosen just that moment to avenge his father's death, for he was thus the means of saving Timoleon's life. He was allowed to go free, and received a gift of gold. The second assassin confessed the plot, and was forgiven.

And now the party of Sicilians who had resisted the advance of Timoleon were so far enraged that they invited the Punic invaders to enter Syracuse. Into the harbor sailed four hundred and fifty ships under the command of Mago, and sixty thousand men of Carthage were landed in the unhappy city. The citadel was still held by Timoleon's men, and he managed to smuggle supplies of corn into the fortress by the hands of brave fellows who, in small fishing-boats, passed through the Punic fleet on a stormy day. But it was perilous to stay in the citadel. The garrison sallied forth, and made themselves secure in a certain quarter of the city, throwing up a strong fence behind which to fight. Soon, with a roar and a rush, the men of Corinth poured into the city, and, without the loss of a single man, Timoleon gained the citadel. For many years the tyrants of Syracuse had used the citadel as a place of strength to awe and cow the citizens.

"Let all the people come hither," was the order of Timoleon, "and lend a hand in overthrowing the walls of this castle of tyrants."

With right good-will did the folk ply pickaxe and crowbar and shovel, and, amid much dust and shouting, the fort was razed to the ground. Afterward, on the self-same spot, they reared a nobler building—a court of justice.

It was time, indeed, for Timoleon to help poor Sicily. The market-place of Syracuse was overgrown with grass, so little trade had been done lately; and in other towns in the islands the wild deer and boars from the forests were roaming unchecked, the people having fled to wild places to hide themselves. At Timoleon's invitation, there came over ten thousand more men from Corinth, to settle in Sicily, and to till the soil and make it yield corn and fruit again.

But the foes from Africa did not readily yield. They sent over a large army in twelve hundred vessels, and some seventy thousand men, with engines to batter city walls, were preparing to conquer the island. Terror seized many Sicilians. Only about five thousand footmen and about one thousand horsemen remained steadfast. Timoleon was not daunted. He led his small army toward a river where he heard the Punic foes were encamped. As he climbed a hill with his troops, he met some mules loaded with parsley.

"A bad sign," murmured the men; "for do we not place parsley on the tombs of the dead?"

"A good sign," cried their leader; "for do we not place crowns of parsley on the heads of those who win races and wrestling-matches?"

Thereupon he made himself a chaplet or wreath of parsley, and crowned his own head.

The river and the marshes that lay about it were at first clad in a thick mist. As the Corinthians paused to take breath on the hilltop after their hard climb, the sun came out and cleared the mist. The enemy were crossing the river. First were seen chariots, each drawn by four horses. Then marched ten thousand warriors carrying white shields, and their helmets were of brass and their breastplates of iron. The Corinthian horsemen darted in and out among the chariots. Timoleon caused his foot-soldiers to draw close together, holding their bucklers in front, so as to make a kind of moving wall.

"Be of good courage!" he cried, in a very loud voice; and the little force descended to the plain.

A tempest burst over the hills and the marshes. Hail beat furiously upon the faces of the Punic foe, and half blinded them while they staggered under the charge of Timoleon's warriors. The victory was to the Corinthians; and more than five thousand prisoners were taken, and heaps of shields and breastplates, captured from the enemy, glittered among the tents of Timoleon's army.

What he did in this battle he did in other places. The invaders were got rid of; the desolate cities were busy with people again; the peasants labored in peace in the field; justice was meted out by the magistrates; and the island of Sicily had cause to bless the name of Timoleon.

He sent for his wife and children from Corinth, and they all dwelt in a country house, where he enjoyed the sweet air of the hills and the sight of harvests and flocks; but his chief happiness was to behold the safety and comfort of the Sicilians.

One day, indeed, at a large public meeting, two noisy talkers made complaints against Timoleon. The people loved the man who had saved the island, and would have risen up in anger and ill-treated the accusers. But Timoleon cried:

"Stay! there is no need for me to answer these men; for what I have done is the best answer. The poorest man in Syracuse can obtain justice, and the citizens enjoy free speech, and each man may speak his mind as he wills."

Alas for Timoleon! He had given liberty to Sicily; but, in his old age, blindness came upon him, and he could no longer take regular part in public affairs. Yet the people still felt deep respect for the blind old man, and many a visitor to Syracuse would ask the way to Timoleon's house if haply he might chance to see the deliverer of Sicily. Sometimes, when the citizens had assembled in the theatre and were unable to decide some troublesome question of government, they would send for Timoleon; and the aged general was borne on a litter through the streets amid the greetings of the crowd.

He died 337 B.C. Great was his funeral. The bier upon which his body lay was grandly adorned, and it was carried by chosen young men across the place where once stood the dreadful citadel of the tyrants. It was followed by a multitude of men and women, who were crowned with flowers and wore white dresses. Many tears were shed by the mourning citizens, and a herald cried with a loud voice:

"The people of Syracuse will bury Timoleon the Corinthian at the public cost; and each year, through all time, they will hold in his honor games at racing and wrestling, while music is played; for he put down tyrants, conquered the foreign invaders, gave welfare to cities that had been laid waste, and restored law and peace to Sicily."

In the market-place was built a pleasant house, in the courts of which the young men of Syracuse might take exercise and engage in sport. It was called the Timoleonteum, or House of Timoleon. And thus, in joyous games, the people remembered the noble soul who gained freedom for a suffering land.

THE ORATOR

"THE sword-maker is dead," said one citizen of Athens to another.

"Has he not left a young son?"

"Yes, the poor child is only seven years of age, and he has no mother."

"Who will look after him?"

"His father chose certain guardians to look after the boy and take charge of the money (for he had gained a big fortune by sword-making), and see to his education."

But I am sorry to say the guardians kept much of the money for themselves, and did not send him to good schools or pay for his being taught at home. So when the lad, whose name was Demosthenes (*Dee-mos-then-eez*), about 384–322 B.C., grew to manhood, he found himself a good deal less learned than other young fellows of his age. He longed to be a speaker to the people—an orator. But his lungs were weak, and so his voice was not strong. Also he had trouble in saying words plainly. He stammered; that is, instead of saying easily such a sentence as, "My dear friends, allow me to remind you," he would say, "My dear friends—ah—my dear friends—hm!—allow me to—ah—ah—ah—to—ah—remind you!" And he could not readily pronounce the letter R, just as some persons in England to-day say "weddy" instead of "ready," and for "blackberries" they say "blackbewies." He made up his mind to improve his style of speech. In an underground cave he fitted up a room where he could read aloud and practise himself in the art of addressing a crowd of people. Perhaps he would eat, drink, and sleep in this strange dwelling for two or three months; and he would shave the hair off one side of his head so that he might not like to go out and show himself to the citizens, and thus he forced himself to stay indoors and study. Sometimes he would watch his reflection in a mirror of polished copper or silver, so that he might note his face and limbs and make sure that his actions were graceful as he spoke. You know some speakers are not graceful, and while they are talking they will scratch their heads, roll their eyes about, or swing their arms.

At other times he would put stones in his mouth and then speak; and, of course, it was a great struggle to pronounce distinctly. If you were to put several pebbles in your mouth and say, "Please, mother, may I have some more marmalade?" your mother would smile at the sounds you made. Though, indeed, some persons that I know speak their words with so little care that you might suppose they always carried pebbles in their mouths. Well, this exercise obliged Demosthenes to utter each syllable with much pains, so that when the stones were taken out he could speak both readily and plainly. Also he would now and then walk along the seashore near Athens, and, on a windy day, when the water rolled noisily on the shingle, he would make a speech as if he were address-ing a disorderly mob of city folk. Another amusing plan was to run up a hill while uttering sentences, so that you might have seen this young man hastening up a mountain-side while he cried aloud: "O, Athenians, it is your duty to defend the temples of the gods; you will be covered with shame if you do not"; and now and then he would sit on a rock to take breath again! Often, when he was about to address the citizens, he would sit up at night, by the glimmer of an oil lamp, writing out and repeating what he meant to say at the meeting; and a man who was jealous of him once sneered:

"Demosthenes, your speeches smell of the lamp!"

In the days of Demosthenes a danger hung over the lovely land of Greece. The danger was in the north, in the kingdom of Macedonia (*Mas-se-do-nia*), which was ruled by King Philip. Bold and strong were the soldiers of Philip, and especially to be feared was their manner of fighting in the phalanx (*fal-anks*). In a phalanx the men formed sixteen ranks, and each held a lance eighteen feet long, pointing it toward the enemy, so that the sixteen rows of warriors, with their great lances, made a dreadful wall for footmen or horsemen to dash against.

Now, it was in the heart of Philip to conquer all the States of Greece—Sparta, Athens, and the rest; and the Greeks were not so willing to fight for their land as their fathers had been. They rather wanted other men to fight for them in return for wages; but these paid armies would not fight so bravely as men who, out of love for their country or city, took up arms and went forth to war. When the troops of King Philip took various towns on the borders of Greece, and were little by little approaching nearer to Athens, Demosthenes tried to waken his countrymen by such words as these:

"The fortune of King Philip has been very great. But the fortune of Athens will be greater still, and she will deserve the help of the kind gods, if only you, Athenians, will do your duty. Yet here you are, sitting still, doing nothing. A sluggard cannot get his friends to work for him, and neither will the gods work for him. I do not wonder that Philip is stronger than you, for he is always in the field, always in movement, doing everything for himself, never letting a chance slip; while you talk, and argue, and vote, but do no soldier-like deeds."

One evening, while the chief magistrates of Athens were at supper together, a messenger ran in from the north to say that King Philip had captured a town on the road to Thebes. All the city were alarmed at the news, for Thebes was a strong town, and its people were known to favor Philip, and if Thebes cast in its lot with the foe, the way of Philip to Athens would be easy. A meeting was held in the market-place as soon as the sun rose the next morning. A herald asked, in a loud voice:

"Who wishes to speak?"

No answer from the vast crowd.

"Who wishes to speak?"

No answer.

At length up rose Demosthenes; and he advised that men be sent to Thebes to persuade the people of that city to join Athens in withstanding the northern king and his terrible phalanxes. Several messengers were sent, and among them was Demosthenes. Messengers from Philip also arrived in Thebes. To which side would the Thebans turn? Philip's messengers spoke of his power, and the strong friendship he would show to such as aided him; and the Thebans cheered loudly at the words. Then Demosthenes spoke, and begged the Thebans to remember they were Greeks, of the same race as the Athenians, and speaking the same noble Greek language, and worshipping the same gods. The Thebans were touched by his pleading; they voted to side with Athens.

Alas! a battle followed, and the power of the phalanx won the victory. A thousand Athenians lay dead, and two thousand were taken captive; and the Thebans lost as many. Demosthenes himself was in this battle, and he had to join in the retreat. When the news came to Athens, the terror was great, and old men, women, and children went up and down in the streets with much outcry.

The walls were made stronger; trees were hastily felled to make new defences; and the fleet was prepared for action. Philip, however, made peace with Athens, and gave up the two thousand prisoners; only he forced Athens to agree that he should be called the

Chief of Greece. When Philip died, his famous son, Alexander, took the lordship of Greece and Macedonia.

Demosthenes was fairly rich, and, at his own expense, he rebuilt the walls of Athens, and the people showed their esteem for him by giving him a crown of gold. It was said by certain of his enemies that he would take the part of any one who would give him gold—that is, bribe him. And once, when Harpalus, the treasure-keeper, fled from Alexander, and came with his bags of money to Athens, some persons whispered that he had bribed Demosthenes to defend his character by the gift of a cup full of golden coins.

Next day, when Demosthenes was asked to come to the public assembly and state what he thought of the dishonest treasurer, he came with woollen wraps about his neck, saying he had a very bad cold, and could not use his voice! Such is the story related in some books; but you must not believe all you read in the books of history; and I think this account of Demosthenes and the cup of gold is not true.

In the year 322, some time after the death of Alexander, the orator returned to Athens from exile, for he had been banished for a while because of the tale of the bribery. The Athenians met the galley that bore him with shouts of joy. But when the Macedonian generals heard of the return of Demosthenes, they sent to arrest him. He fled across the water to an island on which stood a temple to the Sea-god. In this building he hoped to remain in safety. But his enemies came in boats, and demanded to speak with him. They said his life should be spared if he surrendered. He did not trust their promise. Retiring to a chamber of the temple in order to write a letter, he seemed to be biting the pen while he was thinking how to compose. He was, in fact, sucking poison from the hollow of the pen. Presently he rose up as if to walk from the temple, but he fell near the altar and died. In his memory the Athenians set up a statue of brass.

Orators serve their fatherland by speech, as other men serve it by the sword, or, far better, by their daily labor. Demosthenes was the chief orator of Greece; Cicero was an orator in Rome. In England two great orators were the Earl of Chatham and Mr. Gladstone. In America we think readily of Patrick Henry, Henry Clay, and Daniel Webster.

THE CONQUEROR

"Y OU will run in the races, of course?"

"Yes," said the young Prince Alexander; "I will run if I can run with kings."

Alexander had a very high spirit. He showed it also in the affair of the mettlesome horse which had been offered to King Philip for thirteen talents ($12,500). The animal turned fiercely upon the grooms who came near him, and would let no one get astride on his back. King Philip bade the owner take the horse away.

"What a fine creature you are losing," said the young prince, "simply because they have not the skill and spirit to manage him."

"My son," replied his father, "it is easy to find fault, but do you think you could manage him any better yourself?"

"Yes."

"And suppose you failed?"

"I would pay the thirteen talents."

The bystanders laughed. Alexander, by his father's leave, made the trial. He first turned the horse's head toward the sun, so that the steed should not see his own shadow dancing on the ground. Then he stroked him, and spoke gently, and at length leaped on his back, using neither whip nor spur. The horse ran at a great pace, and then Alexander shouted and spurred, and the animal flew. King and onlookers all stood silent until the prince returned in safety. Philip kissed the youth, and cried:

"Seek another kingdom, my son, for Macedonia is too small for thee!"

He did seek another kingdom, for in a few years' time Alexander, who was born 356 B.C., had made himself master of all the known world. In war he showed the same courage and will-power that he had shown in taming the horse. Often did he read the poem of Homer, called the "Iliad" (*Il-i-ad*), which told of the siege of the city of Troy, and of the battles of Greeks and Trojans:

> Now shield with shield, with helmet helmet closed,
> To armor armor, lance to lance opposed,
> Host against host with shadowy squadrons drew,
> The sounding darts in iron tempests flew.

This poem of war Alexander used to put under his pillow, along with a sword, before he slept.

After Philip died Alexander set out to conquer Asia. Already the people of Greece and Macedonia looked upon him as a man of power, for already he had done great deeds in battle. He visited the city of Corinth, where a meeting of Greek captains and statesmen was held. Many men of renown came to see him and say pleasant things. But not Diogenes (*Dy-oj-en-eez*), who was a stern and wise teacher, though he was strange in his manners. So Alexander went to see the philosopher, who often used to lie in a large tub for shelter. I suppose he did that to show folk how small and simple a dwelling a man could live in without any real need of rich furniture and things like that. Diogenes was lying on the ground, enjoying the sunshine.

"Sir," said King Alexander, "I have heard of you as a sage, and have often wished to see you. In what way can I serve you?"

"Only stand a little out of my sunshine," said the philosopher.

"Brute!" said one courtier.

"Wretched rude fellow!" exclaimed another.

Alexander's thoughts were different. He admired the brave man who would not bend the knee to kings.

"If I were not Alexander," he remarked, "I should like to be Diogenes."

Before he left his native land the young king gave away almost all his lands and goods to various friends. Some one said to him:

"You are very free in giving. What have you left for yourself?"

"Hope," said Alexander.

With hope in his heart, Alexander crossed the narrow sea between Europe and Asia, taking with him horses, chariots, and about thirty-five thousand men.

A rapid stream barred the road. On the rocky bank on the opposite side the Persians crowded in thick masses, armed with bow and spear. Through the splash of the river Alexander made his way, and his friends kept close to their leader. On his left arm was strapped a buckler; on his head rested a large helmet, on each side of which waved a white feather. The arrows of the Persians rattled on the shields of the invaders. Persian horsemen rushed down the steep slopes and charged the cavalry of Alexander, and the king's helmet was split by a battle-axe. Just then an officer named Clitus slew the holder of the battle-axe with his spear. Later on in the fight Alexander's horse (not the proud creature of whom I have just told you) was killed under him. The victory lay with the Greeks (for the Macedonians were a kind of Greeks).

In his march toward Persia, Alexander came to the town of Gordium, which he captured. A temple stood there, and in it was kept a chariot, round the pole of which was fastened a rope, very cunningly tied with many knots. The citizens had a saying that "The man who untied the Gordian Knot should have the empire of the world." Alexander pulled at the tangled rope for some time, until he got out of patience. Then he drew his sword and cut the Gordian Knot.

And now Darius (*Da-ry-us*), the sultan, or king, of Persia, had come forth with a host of half a million warriors to meet the Greek foe; and he hoped to deal

Alexander a deadly blow when he met him in the mountains of Cilicia (*Sy-lis-ia*). One army was so large, the other so small, it was like an elephant, at war with a lion. Not long before these two armies clashed together in horrid war, Alexander bathed in a cold stream and took a chill, and lay abed in sore pain, and the soldiers in his camp felt great fear lest their master should die. Nor were any of the medical men in the army able to heal his sickness. They were afraid to give him drugs which might not cure, and then the wrath of the army would fall upon them. But one physician, whose name was Philip, held Alexander in much love, and he also desired, for the sake of the people, to save the king's life. Therefore, he said he would prepare a drink which would send the king to sleep, and on waking he would feel much relief from his illness. The king agreed.

While the potion (or drink) was being mixed by the careful hands of Philip, the sick king received a letter from one of his friends. It read thus:

Sir, beware of the man Philip. The King of Persia has promised to give him much gold, and also a princess for wife, if he will poison you.

Alexander smiled as he read this note. He did not believe it was true, and he thrust it under his pillow. Presently the physician gave him the cup. The king handed the letter to Philip and began to drink. As the king sipped the potion he watched the face of Philip. The physician read the cruel words. He looked angry, and then:

"Oh, sir," he cried, as he knelt by the royal bedside, "you surely do not think I would be so base as to do you this harm?"

Alexander shook his head, and went to sleep. It was a long, long sleep, and the officers of the army came in from time to time to gaze at the kingly sleeper's pale features. Perhaps the writer of the letter came and glanced darkly at Philip. But the king awoke; his fever had waned, his blood was cooler, and the camp was filled with joy.

The battle took place soon afterward, and the huge forces of Darius melted away before the onset of the phalanxes of Alexander. We may say that already was Alexander master of Persia. Darius fled in a chariot, leaving behind him his wife and daughters and his treasures. The Macedonians took of the spoil, each man for himself; but they kept the tent of the Persian king for their leader. It was a large and splendid tent, hung with curtains, and containing gold and silver boxes, and vases, and dishes, and other precious things. Alexander stood for a while gazing silently at the glittering heap, and then he said:

"And so this is being a king!"

He smiled as he spoke the words, for well he knew that kingship did not lie in having piles of jewels and rare objects, but in wise thoughts and valiant deeds. And it is the same with men who are not kings. A man's worth is not to be reckoned by the valuable coat he wears or the rich villa he dwells in. We may dress an ape in cloth of gold, and he will still be an ape.

The unhappy ladies left by the King of Persia wondered what evil fate would now come upon them. They were much comforted by a message from Alexander saying that they were not to fear, for he would bid his soldiers pay all respect to them. Placed in a tent by themselves, with women to serve them as in the brighter days now past, the Persian queen and princesses were treated with honor. Alexander was a man of noble temper. When he behaved so fairly and courteously to the women he was chivalrous, and all boys and men ought to be like him. To be chivalrous means to act with respect toward women, and especially toward women who are weak and need help.

Early one morning the army of King Alexander was astir. Chariot-horses were being harnessed; footmen strapping their armor on; cavalrymen were mounting.

"Fire!" cried a soldier.

A fire was burning near the king's tent, but when the men ran up no one was allowed to throw water. The flames leaped in and out of a large heap of clothes, boxes, all sorts of valuable goods. It was the baggage of the king and his friends.

"Why is the king burning the luggage?" was the question asked by every one.

The king replied:

"Because we are going to India. The march will be a heavy one. We shall need all our strength to meet the dangers and hindrances of the journey. We do not want to be burdened with this spoil."

The army thought the king was right. Each man brought to the fire whatever he did not really need, and so the Macedonians set out for India with a very light baggage.

On the way they attacked a castle which stood on the top of a steep hill. Among the band of Greeks who were to lead the onset was a young fellow named Alexander. King Alexander said to the young soldier Alexander:

"You must bear yourself bravely, my friend, in order to do justice to your name."

And he did; and the king heard with much pleasure that the young warrior had behaved as a man named Alexander should.

All you girls and boys who read this page have the names of your parents—Taylor, Smith, Johnson, Wood, and so on. And all these names are good names; and so you must act in a way that is worthy of the name borne by your mother and your father.

Another fortress which the army lay siege to was protected by a river.

"What a wretch am I," cried Alexander, "that I did not learn to swim!"

Not a wretch, indeed; but the king had the sense to confess that he had left undone a thing which he ought to have done.

Well, before the assault had gone far a group of men came out of the fort and asked to see the Greek king, for they wished to make an offer to surrender the place. A meeting was arranged, and servants brought the king a couch. He at once invited the oldest of the visitors to take a seat, while he himself stood—a good example of the thoughtful manner in which younger people should treat the aged.

Dreadful was the battle which Alexander fought with the Indian Prince Porus. This Indian was very tall, and he rode on the back of a very large elephant. Many of his followers were also mounted on these huge beasts. Greek courage did not flinch before the Indian elephants or the Indian arrows. The elephant on which Porus was carried fought with a most determined spirit, as if it knew that India and the prince were in danger. At length it knelt, for the prince was sore wounded, and must needs dismount, and yield himself prisoner to the foe.

"How do you wish me to treat you?" asked Alexander.

"As a king," replied Porus.

"But have you nothing more to ask?"

"No, it is all summed up in the word king."

Alexander, who was brave himself, admired other men who were brave. Pleased with the Indian's answer, he gave him back all his land, which he was to rule as governor under the chief kingship of Alexander. In the midst, however, of this great triumph, a sadness came upon the Greek king. The faithful horse, of whose taming I have told you the story, died at the age of thirty, and was buried with great respect.

Many of the Macedonians died in India. The army would not march farther into that far land. Alexander at first shut himself up in his tent, and would speak to no man, so deep was his grief. At last he gave way to the will of the soldiers, and began the return journey to the West. For seven months he and his followers sailed down the big river Indus, stopping here and there to fight with the natives on the banks. Then the Greek warriors tramped a weary march along the shore of the Persian gulf; over sand, dust, stones; under the hot sun; in a region where little food could be got. For sixty days the distress lasted. When the army passed from this dry and hopeless land they rested awhile, and then, for seven days, went forward by easy marches in a kind of procession, as if on a holiday. The king was drawn in his chariot by eight horses. So large was the royal chariot that it was covered with a broad wooden platform, on which tables could be placed; and here Alexander and his friends, crowned with flowers, sat eating and drinking (especially drinking). Many other chariots came in the train of the king's, some being adorned with purple hangings, others with branches of trees. The soldiers tripped along to the sound of flutes and clarionets. They sang loud songs; and often they stayed to dip their cups in open tubs of wine which the king had provided.

And so they danced, and so they drank, and so they sang. But Alexander had a different feeling in his heart when, on coming back to Persia, he arrived at the grave of the famous King Cyrus. On a slab of stone over the tomb were cut these words, which the King of Macedon read: "O man, whoever you are, and no matter where you come from, I who lie here am

CYRUS, the founder of the Persian Empire. Do not envy me the little earth that covers my body."

A long time did Alexander stand still, after reading these words; for they made him think how soon the great power of kings may vanish away.

Alexander had a dear friend named Hephæstion (*Hef-eest-yon*), who fell sick of a fever. The doctor bade the sick man keep from rich food. But, while the medical man was away enjoying a play at the theatre, the patient ate a roast fowl and drank a large jug of cold wine. A few days after this foolish act he died. Alexander was thrown into a dreadful sorrow. All the horses and mules in the army had their hair shorn in token of mourning, and the doctor was nailed to a cross and crucified. Not a sound of music was allowed in the camp for a long time; and, in his mad grief, the king bade that all prisoners taken in the wars should be slain. I fear, indeed, that the mind of this wonderful king and conqueror was touched with strange disorder. He had led the Greeks from Greece to India. He had made the people of the East bow before the might of the people of the West. He had broken the rule of the proud kings of Persia, who had so often marched armies to the West, and tried to make slaves of the Greeks. And where the Greeks went they took their books and poetry and music, and so gave new ideas and new manners to the folk who were less learned than themselves. But these deeds had puffed up Alexander's soul with pride. He became vain, and he became more selfish than he once had been. He had conquered the world, but he could not conquer himself. Soon he would lose his kingship.

One day he had gone to the bath, and, after washing, he clad himself in a light dress, and played at ball with some young men. When he had played all he wanted he bade his comrades fetch his clothes. They entered the throne-chamber, and there they saw a strange man, dressed in Alexander's robes, seated on the throne, wearing the crown, and looking dreamily in front of him, speaking never a word. He was not right in his mind, and was removed and put to death.

Ah, but the king himself would not sit many more times on the throne. He had now reached the city of Babylon. A fever seized him. When he felt the illness coming on he would not take care for his health, but, like the friend of whom I have told you, he swallowed deep draughts of wine. Now and then he seemed much better, and he would lie on his couch and listen to the stories related by the admiral of the fleet. The king had sent a fleet of ships to sail along the coasts of Persia and Arabia, and the sunburnt sailor had seen the wonders of the Indian Ocean. After Alexander had been sick twenty-five days the soldiers took alarm. They crowded about the house where he lay. They must see him. So they were allowed to enter his chamber, in long lines, walking softly past the bed where the conqueror's pale face turned uneasily on the pillow. One evening, in the month of June, in the year 323 B.C., Alexander the Great died, only thirty-three years of age.

A SERVANT OF THE CITY

"I BELIEVE," said one soldier to another, "that we are going to have a sharp winter."

"What makes you think so?"

"The general has his cloak on."

"That is nothing unusual, is it?"

"Yes, for Phocion (*Fose-yon*) is a hardy man, and never wears more clothes than he really needs. And he always goes barefoot."

If you had looked at Phocion, the Athenian general, you would have thought him harsh and stern. But his heart was kind and just. One day a speaker was addressing a crowd of Athenians, and he pointed to the general, and made a joke about his frowning forehead.

"My friends," said Phocion, "this brow of mine never gave you one hour of sorrow, while the men who have smiled as they spoke to you have brought Athens to tears."

Poor Athens! this fair city by the sea had many a trouble to bear at this time. It was the time when the Greeks of the north—the stout warriors of Macedonia—were becoming masters of the neighboring lands; the time of King Philip and of Alexander the Great. Phocion did not think the men of Athens were strong enough and wise enough to keep free; he thought it would be better for them to own the Macedonians as their leaders and lords. The Athenians loved to gather in the streets, and shout as they listened to orators who pleased them; but they were not ready to work hard in the defence of the State. Once, when the citizens cried out for war against another Greek State, Phocion said: "Let us rather settle the quarrel by peaceable means."

"No, no," yelled the mob; "to arms! to arms!"

"My good people," replied the general, "you had better keep to the style you understand most, and that is talking, not fighting."

He himself, though he talked only in short and quiet sentences, was not backward in war. As a young man he had taken part in a naval battle, and did much to gain victory for the ships of Athens. And so great faith had the citizens in his courage and good sense that, during his long life, 402–317 B.C., he was chosen general forty-five times; and yet he never asked to be elected.

When he was sent to certain islands to ask the people to pay their share to the expenses of the city of Athens, he was advised to take twenty war-vessels with him, so as to make him seem a man of power.

"If," said Phocion, "I am to cow these folk, I ought to take more ships. If I go to them as to friends, one galley is enough."

He sailed, therefore, with but one ship. So respectfully did he talk with the people of the islands that they, in their turn, showed him honor, and gave him the money which he asked for in the name of Athens. Thus did he prove himself to be a good statesman; for, though he would fight when he saw reason to do so, he sought rather to gain people by a courteous manner.

News came to Athens that King Philip was dead, and some of the citizens wanted to hold a holiday in token of their pleasure, for they hated Philip.

"No," said Phocion, "it is a mean thing to show joy at the death of an enemy."

Of course, if Philip was an enemy to Athens, you could not expect the citizens to show sorrow at his death. But it was not meet to break out into mirth and cheer because a brave foe had passed away.

After Philip came Alexander; and the young king, knowing that Phocion was friendly to Macedonia, thought to please him with a gift of money. Messengers came to Phocion's house, bearing a hundred talents ($100,000). Everything about the place was simple and plain. The wife was baking bread.

"Phocion," she said, "I want some water."

The Athenian general took a bucket and drew water from the well. When he had done this and other tasks, he sat down and wiped the dust from his bare feet. This was unusual. Men who were in high position such as he was in would bid slaves wash their feet for them.

PHOCION & THE MACEDONION ENVOY

"Sir," said one of the Macedonians, "you are Alexander's friend, and the friend of a king ought not to live in so shabby a style."

Just then a poor old man, in patched garments, passed by the door.

"Do you think I am worse off than that old man?" asked Phocion.

"No, sir."

"Well, but he lives on much less than I do, and is content. I should feel no happier if I had Alexander's money."

The messengers carried the talents back to Macedonia.

I have told you that Phocion was forty-five times chosen general of the Athenian army. Just when he had been elected on the twentieth occasion, a lady called to see his wife, and showed to the simple woman her necklaces and bracelets.

"And now let me see your jewels," said the visitor.

"Phocion is my ornament," answered Phocion's wife; "he has just been chosen for the twentieth time for the command of the Athenian army."

The son of the general, however, was not so fine in spirit as his father and mother. Phocus (*Fokus*) was the young man's name. He had given way to drinking, and his father persuaded him to take part in the sports, especially the foot-races. Phocus trained himself, and ran in a race and won; and one of his friends made a great feast in his honor. Phocion came to the house where the feast was going on, and was much vexed to see the waste, for the guests that entered sat down and had their feet bathed in spiced wine. The general called his son to him, and thus reproached him:

"My son, why do you let your friends spoil the honor of your victory? You won the race by being temperate, and now you are wasting your strength in riotous living."

Not even when he was aged would Phocion resign his service. A stir was made in Athens against the people of a neighboring State, and the crowd shouted for war. So Phocion bade a herald proclaim in the streets:

"All citizens who are under the age of sixty are to enroll themselves in the army, and take with them food to last five days, and follow me at once to the camp."

But many of the elder men did not relish the order, and, instead of following the herald, began to move homeward.

"Why are you troubled?" cried Phocion. "Do you think you are too old for the wars? I myself, though I am eighty years old, will be your leader."

Thereupon the elder men, who dared not say they were not young enough, put on their armor and followed Phocion, and a victory was gained.

But the power of Athens was becoming less. Though King Alexander was dead, the Macedonians were, step by step, stretching their lordship over the Greek States; and the people of Athens watched the new masters come nearer and nearer; and, though they bragged loudly, they did not feel bold enough to withstand the men of the north. One day a priest was kneeling by the edge of the harbor washing a pig, and suddenly a shark rushed forward and bit off a part of the pig's body.

"Alas!" said the seers, or fortune-tellers, "this means that a part of Athens will be lost."

Shortly afterward a band of Macedonian soldiers entered Athens and took possession of the lower portion of the city near the sea. There was no fighting. The new garrison said they came as friends; but the Athenian folk knew in their hearts that the freedom of the city was gone. And then they turned in anger upon the good old general, who had for so many years served the city and fought for it and helped to govern it. Phocion was arrested as an enemy of the State—a traitor.

Phocion and some of his friends were placed in an open-air theatre, where a vast crowd of people had gathered, and they voted, with a loud shout, that Phocion and his companions must die. And some persons even placed garlands of flowers upon their heads, as if they were doing a happy deed. Then was Phocion led away to the jail; and as he went certain men abused him with evil words, and one even spat upon him. He showed no anger, but turned to the magistrates, and said:

"Will none of you chide this fellow for his rudeness?"

At the prison they found the jailer mixing the hemlock poison in a bowl for the condemned men to drink. One of the party begged Phocion to let him drink first. "For," said he, "I do not want to see you die."

"It is a hard request," replied Phocion; "but as I have always tried to oblige you in life, I will also do so in death. Drink before me."

And thus Phocion, the patriot, died with his friends. A sound of trampling steeds was heard. It was a train of horsemen that passed by the prison. They were keeping holiday, and their heads were crowned with flowers. But many shed quiet tears as they went by, for they thought of the good general whose voice they would hear no more.

And afterward the people were sorry for the deed they had done, and they raised up a statue of brass in his memory.

But the city of Athens was never again free.

GOLDEN SHOES AND TWO CROWNS

KINGS dream, just as other people do. A King of Macedon (*Mass-e-don*) dreamed that he was a sower, and he went forth to sow gold-dust. After a while he went to the field, and found corn growing that had golden ears. After a while again he went, and, alas! he saw the corn cut. Some man had been and cut the shining crop, and left nothing but useless stalks. And he heard a voice say: "Prince Mithridates (*Mith-ri-day-teez*) has stolen the golden corn and gone away toward the Black Sea."

The king told his son Demetrius (*Dee-mee-tri-us*), who lived from about 338 B.C. to 283 B.C. "I shall kill Mithridates," he said; "we have let him stay at our palace all this time as a friend, and he has gone hunting with you and enjoyed himself. But now I feel sure, according to my dream, that he means harm to you and me."

Of course, you know the king was wrong. He had no right to hurt the prince because of the bad dream. Dreams cannot give us wise warnings, though I know some foolish books are printed which pretend to tell fortunes by dreams.

The heart of young Demetrius was sad at the thought of the danger that was coming upon his companion. He had, however, promised the king that he would not speak a word on the subject.

"Well," he whispered to himself, "it is true I promised not to speak, but I can tell my friend of the peril without speaking!"

Soon afterward, while they were out sporting with other youths, Demetrius drew the prince to one side, and wrote on the ground with the end of his spear these two words:

"Fly, Mithridates."

The prince understood at once. As soon as darkness came on he fled, and took passage in a galley across the Black Sea to his native land in Asia Minor.

You see that Demetrius was ready to help a friend in need; but I fear I cannot tell very much that is good of him, for, above all things, he was a man of war. While he was yet a very young man he went to and fro in Asia, waging war against the Arabs, from whom he once captured seven hundred camels; or against various Greek princes. For you must know that after the death of Alexander the Great large lands in Asia, Egypt, etc., were shared among his captains, so that there were Greek rulers over many foreign countries.

He resolved to go to the aid of Athens. The castle at Athens was held by a band of men who, though they were Greeks, were tyrants over the city. Demetrius sailed with a fleet of two hundred and fifty ships. The people did not know he was coming. They saw the fleet, but supposed that it belonged to their masters. No guard was set at the mouth of the harbor, and the galleys of Demetrius entered without a fight. A multitude of people ran to the landing-place, and saw the young prince on board his ship. He made signs to them to keep silence. Then a herald shouted from the prince's ship in a very loud voice:

"O ye people of Athens, be it known to you that the Prince Demetrius has come to give you your freedom, to drive out your foes, and to restore the good old laws and government that your city once possessed."

A great shout went up from the Athenian folk, and Demetrius landed with his men. He laid siege to the fortress, and soon mastered it.

Near Athens was a town which the prince also attacked. His soldiers burst in, and began to plunder the houses. But he remembered that in this town there lived a wise man—a philosopher—named Stilpo—a man who lived a quiet life and studied, and loved knowledge more than he loved money. So Demetrius sent to Stilpo's house, and bade his soldiers fetch the sage to his presence.

"Have my men robbed anything from you?" asked the prince.

"No," answered Stilpo; "none of your men want to steal knowledge, and that is all I have."

It may amuse you to hear how one of the prince's friends took the news of a victory to the old

King of Macedon. Demetrius fought with one hundred and eighty ships against one hundred and fifty ships of the King of Egypt (this king was also a Greek). Seventy of the enemy's vessels were captured, many others were sunk, and the King of Egypt escaped with only eight. After the battle, Demetrius behaved nobly. He set all the prisoners free, and he gave decent burial to all the enemy's dead. A messenger was sent to Macedon with the tidings. This messenger ordered the ship that carried him to anchor off the coast, while he went ashore in a small boat. Alone he landed; alone he walked toward the palace of the king. Some one ran up to him from the king.

"What is the news?"

No answer.

Another, and another; but they received no reply. The aged king, in much alarm, came to the door, and the people crowded round. Then the messenger stretched out his hand, and cried:

"Hail to thee, O king! We have totally beaten the King of Egypt at sea; we are masters of the island of Cyprus."

"Hail to thee, also, my good friend," said the king; "but you have kept us waiting a long time, and I shall keep you waiting before I give you any reward for your news."

Demetrius had a great love for making ships. He built galleys that were worked by fifteen or sixteen banks of oars—that is, the men sat in fifteen or sixteen rows, making in all, perhaps, one hundred and twenty oarsmen, all pulling together. Demetrius would stand on the beach watching his galleys sweep by. Another thing he liked to build was a machine for besieging a fortress. It was like a huge cart in the shape of a tower, rolling on four large wheels or rollers, each wheel sixteen feet high. The tower was divided into stages or floors, one above the other. On each of these stages stood armed men, ready to throw stones, darts, etc., at the people on the walls of the besieged fortress. As the tower was pushed toward the fort the wheels creaked, the men shouted, and great was the terror of it!

Of course, after the old king's death Demetrius became King of Macedon. Ships and siege-towers were more interesting to him than giving justice to the people. He wore two crowns on his head, his robe was purple, and his feet were shod with cloth of gold.

One day he walked in the street, and some persons gave him petitions, or rolls of paper on which their requests were written. He put them in a fold of his cloak till he came to a bridge, and then he pitched all the rolls into the river! But an old woman fared better on another occasion. She begged him to listen to her story of trouble. "I have no time," he replied, shortly.

"Then," cried the dame, "you should not be a king!"

These words struck home to his soul. On arriving at his palace, he put aside all other business, and ordered that every person who wished to see him about wrongs they had suffered should be admitted. The old woman was brought to him first, and he listened to her tale, and punished the man who had evil-treated her. And to others also he did justice, sitting in his royal chair day after day for the purpose. But it was only now and then that he acted in this kingly way. Too often his mind was given to war, to sieges, attacks, and conquests.

His last war was waged among the rocky hills and passes of Syria. Nearly all his warriors deserted him, and went over to the side of his enemy. Demetrius and a few friends took refuge in a forest, and waited till night fell and the stars glittered above the mountains. They crept out of the forest and across the rocks, but saw the camp-fires of the foe on every hand. All hope was gone. Demetrius gave himself up as a prisoner of war. For three years he was confined in a Syrian castle, and was allowed to go hunting in a large park, to walk in the gardens, and to feast royally with his companions. After a time he lost his fiery spirit and cared naught for the pleasures of the chase. He drank deep from the wine-cup, and gambled with his money and worked harm to his health, and died at the age of fifty-four, in the year 283 B.C.

His body having been burned after the manner of the Greeks, the ashes that remained were put into an urn of gold. The urn was set on a raised part of the deck of a galley, and armed men sat in the ship. Slowly the vessel was rowed across the sea, while a skilful flute-player sounded a sweet and solemn air. The oars kept time to the notes of the flute. The son of Demetrius came to meet the funeral-galley with a fleet of many ships; and thus the urn of gold was taken to the port of Corinth, and thence it was carried to a tomb.

UP THE SCALING-LADDERS

"CHILD! where did you come from?" asked a woman of a seven-year-old boy whom she found in her house.

"Lady, take pity on me. If I am seen in the street, the soldiers of the tyrant may slay me. They have killed my father. I fled from the horrid noise and the sight of blood, and I wandered here and there till I saw your open door, and I entered."

"Do not tremble. I will take care of you till dark, and then one of my friends shall guide you to the city of Argos, where many people have gone so as to escape the tyrant's wrath."

The name of the lad was Aratus (*A-ray´-tus*), and the city where he was born, 271 B.C., was called Sikyon, and the city had fallen into the power of a tyrant.

A tyrant is a ruler who does what he wills, and takes no heed of the wishes of the people.

At Argos the boy was brought up by kinsmen of his dead father. In his heart there burned a deep hatred of tyrants. If ever he grew to be a man, he would fight against the cruel lord of Sikyon, and any other ruler in any other city who robbed the people of their freedom.

One day Aratus met a man who had escaped from the jail in Sikyon, where he had been shut up for rebelling against the tyrant's rule. He told Aratus how he had come over the wall of the castle and down the cliff and through a garden, and so out on the country road to Argos. It would be possible for a party of men to scale the wall by means of ladders, and so make their way into the fort. But in the garden at the foot of the cliff was the gardener's house, and in it were kept a number of watch-dogs who barked at the least sound. Aratus resolved to climb the wall and capture the fort. A carpenter who had once dwelt in Sikyon made several scaling-ladders, and Aratus collected about a hundred men to attack the castle.

The moon was shining when he and his party started out, but it had set by the time they reached the garden. A few of his followers had gone in front and made the gardener prisoner, but they could not seize the dogs. The ladders were placed against the rocky wall. Men climbed to a ledge, and then drew up the ladders and climbed again. Meanwhile the gardener's dogs yelped very loudly. The ladders shook, and some hearts feared; but Aratus would not go back. With about fifty men he arrived at the top of the rock. It was now near dawn. A flash of light was seen. It was the company of the guard who were coming off duty. They carried torches, and talked as they passed along the broad path along the battlements. Little did they think that Aratus and his men were hanging silently on to the rocks on the other side of the wall. The new guard also marched past, but did not notice anything unusual. Then Aratus got over the wall, followed by his friends, and they ran across the castle-yard to the tyrant's palace, and surprised the soldiers there, and took them all prisoners without any bloodshed. One of his men ran to several houses where lived persons who would be glad to know that Aratus had come. Soon a crowd had gathered from all sides, and they swarmed into the open-air theatre just as the sun was rising. A herald mounted a high place and cried aloud:

"Aratus calls the people to liberty!"

Then they raised a mighty cheer, and rushed to the tyrant's palace and set it on fire. The tyrant fled through underground passages, and so got away. Aratus ordered the fire to be put out. Not one person had been slain in this assault. More than five hundred citizens who had been obliged to leave because of the tyrant's conduct came back to Sikyon. Some had been absent fifty years, and they found their lands in possession of new owners; and it was no easy matter for Aratus to do justice and render them back their property, and yet not do wrong to the new holders of the lands. He formed a court of judges; he himself and fifteen other citizens sitting there to judge the questions and restore the lands to the rightful owners, and paying money to the persons who were turned out. But not having money enough, he thought he would go across to the King of Egypt. This king was friendly to Aratus, and Aratus had sent him many fine paintings done by Greek artists. On the voyage the ship was driven into a Greek port, held by a prince who was a foe to him. He hastened from the vessel and took shelter in a thick wood near the city. The governor of the port seized the ship and its crew, and kept a sharp lookout for Aratus, who concealed himself for several days. By good hap a Roman ship sailed that way, and put in for a while at a cove near the wood. Aratus begged the captain to let him go on board; and in this ship he voyaged to the south coast of Asia Minor, and thence he made passage in another vessel to Egypt. The King of Egypt gave Aratus much gold, and with this he returned to his native city of Sikyon. A number of Greek cities had now joined together to help each other, and they called their union the Achæan (*A-kee-an*) League; and Aratus was chosen general of the League; and many a time did he take part in the wars as leader of these cities.

The famous town of Corinth, a seaside place, was also delivered from a tyrant by the noble Aratus. With four hundred men he marched one night toward Corinth. The moon glittered on their armor, and had it not been for clouds rising and darkening the sky, the Achæans might have been observed. With the aid of the scaling-ladders they mounted the wall, and dropped over into the city. Then they marched quietly, spear in hand. A party of four watchmen met them; three were cut down; the fourth was wounded in the head, but he got free, and cried: "The enemy! the enemy is in the city!" Trumpets were blown. People hurried from their houses with flaming torches. A band of three hundred Achæans had entered Corinth by one of the gates, and had put to flight a troop of the defenders. Meantime Aratus had climbed the rough road that led up to the inner keep or citadel, which was held by the tyrant's men. The three hundred joined him. The moon shone out again, and the walls were stormed amid shouts and the hurling of darts. By the hour of sunrise the keep was captured. The citizens assembled in the theatre; and when Aratus appeared on the stage, and stood silent, leaning on his spear, they applauded their deliverer again and again. The governor had fled.

Aratus also tried to set free the city of Argos, which had yielded to the enemy. Having climbed the ramparts by the help of his ladders, he fought valiantly, and was stabbed in the thigh, and was obliged to retire unsuccessful.

He could bear defeat without losing heart. He also knew how to wait. An army of foes having invaded the land of the League, Aratus would not at once pursue them, but he watched them go by. His men urged him to pursue, but he made no move till he heard that the enemy had taken the city of Pellene (*Pel-ee-nee*). Great was the distress of this city. Houses had been plundered, poor women were dragged shrieking along the streets. One lady was seized by an officer and placed in a temple; and so that all who passed might know she was now his slave, he clapped his helmet on her head. It was a helmet which bore three waving plumes. And now came Aratus with his eager Achæans, and a battle raged in the city streets. The captive lady, hearing the fresh noise, came to the porch of the temple; and as she stood there, handsome and stately, and wearing the feathered helmet, the enemy were struck with terror, for they took her for a goddess who had come to threaten them with ruin; and they gave way in disorder, and Aratus had saved yet another city.

Aratus judged that the League would be stronger if they joined their power with Philip, King of Macedon (not the Philip who was the father to Alexander the Great). But Philip was a mean man and a pretender, and though he seemed friendly to Aratus, really desired to insure his death. He gained his purpose. One of his friends poisoned the food of the brave general, and Aratus died, 213 B.C.

The people of Sikyon were allowed to bury their beloved citizens inside their walls. In his memory they decided to hold two holidays every year. One was on the date when he saved the city from the tyrant, and they called it Salvation Day; and the other was on his birthday. On each occasion a sacrifice was offered to the gods. The folk walked in procession—first boys and young men; then the elders of the senate; then a crowd of citizens; and, to the sound of harps, hymns were sung by a choir. For very many years these festivals were kept up by the grateful people of Sikyon.

And, girls and boys, if ever you see wrong done in the world by rich men, or by statesmen, or governments, you will, I hope, resist the evil thing with hearts as bold as that of Aratus, who scaled the cliffs and feared no tyrant on the face of the earth.

A FIGHTING KING

T HE river ran by with a roar. Gray twilight covered the earth. "There are some men on the other side of the river," said one of the women; "talk to them."

"Ho-o-o-o-o!" shouted the young man. "Help us across the water. We have the little prince Pyrrhus (*Pir-rus*) with us. The enemy are pursuing us!"

"Hi-i-i-i-i!" came back the answer from the farther bank. But neither party could hear the words of the other.

At length one of the young men tore a strip of bark from a tree, and, with a sharp piece of iron, he scratched a few words on the bark, saying that he and his friends were guarding the nurses of the infant prince, whom they had rescued from a tyrant. He tied the bark to a stone, and flung it across the stream. One of the people on the opposite side read it to his comrades. When they understood what was the matter, they made haste to cut down trees and tie the logs together to make a raft—there being no bridge in that place—and soon the nurses, the prince, and their guards were safe over, and were lodged in the town. Thence they travelled to the royal palace in a neighboring country. They found the king and queen sitting among the courtiers, and at the feet of the queen (who was a kinswoman of the infant prince) they laid the child. Young Pyrrhus, who was born about 318 B.C., did not know he had been in danger; he looked up and saw the king's face, and caught hold of his robe, and smiled. The king had been pondering whether he should assist little Pyrrhus or not, for he might bring trouble on himself by doing so. The child's smile touched his heart.

"Yes," he said, "I will take care of the prince of Epirus" (*Ep-py-rus*). Epirus was a hilly land, north of Greece and bordering on the sea by Italy. When he was twelve years old his friends made him king. He was only seventeen years of age when he was again driven from the throne, and he spent some time in fighting battles in Asia. Then he returned to his fatherland. The one thing he seemed to live for was war. He longed to be a mighty captain. As soon as one war was done, he began another; and though he was often beaten, he never shrank from fighting again. His soldiers called him the Eagle, because he moved so swiftly and attacked so boldly.

"If I am an eagle," he replied to them, "you have made me one; for by the help of your spears and swords, and on your wings, have I risen so high."

You see he was quick in his wit. And I will give you an instance of his good-humor.

Some young men were brought before him to explain why they had spoken ill of the king while they sat drinking at a supper.

"Did you really say these bad things about me?" asked Pyrrhus.

"We did, sir," answered one, "and we should have said worse things about you if we had had more wine."

The king laughed and let them go, for he liked the frank and open reply.

He set his mind on pitting his strength against the Romans, for at this time (about 280 B.C.) the men of Rome were becoming very powerful through Italy, and they had it in their minds to conquer the island of Sicily, and many another broad land beyond.

Just before they went aboard the fleet a friend said to him:

"The Romans are excellent soldiers. But suppose, sir, that we beat them, what shall we do then?"

"We shall go up and down Italy, and every town will surrender to us."

"And what next, sir?"

"Next we shall make ourselves masters of the fruitful isle of Sicily."

"Will that be the end?"

"No, for we shall then be ready to cross the sea and capture the famous city of Carthage, in Africa."

"Very good, sir; and what after that?"

"I shall march against Macedonia, a country which I have long wished to add to my domain."

"Yes, sir, and what then?"

"Then I will conquer Greece."

"And after that, sir?"

"Oh, after that we shall take our ease, eat, drink, and be merry."

"Well, sir, but had we not better take our ease, eat, drink, and be merry now, instead of going through all these battles and hardships by land and water?"

No, King Pyrrhus loved the joy of battle (though it was a bad joy), and he was too restless to stay in his own home and look after the comfort of his own people. So he sailed for Italy in many galleys with twenty thousand foot-soldiers, three thousand cavalry, two thousand archers, five hundred slingers, and twenty elephants. A fierce storm smote the fleet on its way, and many a battleship went down with all on board. The king, thinking his army was lost, flung himself into the waves. Several of his friends plunged in after him, and rescued him from the foaming waters, and he lay all night, sick and faint, on the deck of his galley. The day broke; the coast of Italy was in sight; the soldiers landed with the horses and elephants, and the heart of Pyrrhus beat with hope once more.

At first the Romans were defeated. Brave though they were, they were struck with a new fear at the sight of the elephants, who carried little towers on their backs, and waved their trunks and snorted. Such animals had never been seen in Italy. The King of Epirus pressed on, and came within forty miles of the gates of Rome. He sent a messenger to summon the

Romans to yield. The messenger entered the senate-house, where, on benches, sat two or three hundred elder men in council. It was the senate which governed Rome. An old Latin motto was: *Senatus populusque Romanus*, which means, "The Senate and the Roman People."

Some of the senators said it would be better to make peace with Pyrrhus, and most of them began to think this was wise advice. A bustle was heard at the door. An old man was carried in on a chair. His name was Appius, and he was blind.

"Gentlemen," he cried, as he raised his hands, "I have often felt sad because I was blind; but now I wish I was deaf as well as blind; for then I should not be able to hear Romans talk of bowing down before the enemies of their country."

The old man's spirit set all hearts aglow, and the senate voted that the war should be kept going. The messenger went back to Pyrrhus, and told him the Roman senate was an assemblage of kings.

A Roman general named Fabricius (Fab-ris´-yus) was sent to the enemy's camp to arrange for the exchange of prisoners—that is, for every hundred prisoners set free by the enemy the Romans would set free a hundred men of Epirus, and so on. King Pyrrhus had a long talk with this Roman captain, and was pleased with the conversation, and offered him a large sum of gold, which was refused. Next day the king thought to strike terror into the Roman's soul. He ordered that the largest of the elephants should be placed behind a curtain of the room where he and

Fabricius were to consult. A signal was given, the curtain fell, the elephant lifted its trunk and made a fearful trumpeting noise. The Roman looked up without flinching, and then, turning with a smile to the king, he said:

"Neither your gold yesterday nor your beast to-day has power to move me."

Such was the manliness of Romans.

Some time later, when Fabricius was consul (or chief magistrate) of Rome, a letter came to him from the physician of Pyrrhus, offering for money to poison the king, and so rid the Romans of a troublesome foe. Fabricius had too noble a temper to take part in so mean a plot, and he sent the letter to Pyrrhus. When the king had read it he punished the traitor, and then, to show his admiration of the generous act of the consul, he set free all his Roman prisoners. Well, that was excellent; but what a pity it is men cannot see that when warriors do noble things it is the noble spirit that is good, and not the fighting; and when wars have come to an end forever, men will still know how to act fairly and honorably toward each other.

The battles began again. In one engagement, which lasted all day till sunset, each side lost heavily. The friends of Pyrrhus said he had gained a great victory. But he looked at the heaps of the dead, and answered:

"If we gain another victory such as this, we shall be lost."

And that is why we call a battle by which little is gained a Pyrrhic victory.

At last he was forced to leave Italy, and then to leave Sicily, and so he took ship and carried his beaten army—what there was left of it—to Epirus. But he could not rest. He made war on the city of Sparta. Round the city he drew his army, and the citizens prepared to resist to the death. The Spartans had thought of sending the women to a place of safety miles away. But one lady entered the council-chamber with a sword in her hand, and declared that the women would stay in the city and share the lot of the men. When the Spartans built up mounds of earth to prevent the foes from coming in, the women worked hard in piling up the new wall, and I am glad to say the city was not taken, and Pyrrhus retired.

His last campaign was against the Greek city of Argos. One night the gate of Argos was left open by a traitor, and Pyrrhus entered with a crowd of soldiers and a number of elephants, and got as far as the market-place. In the darkness, however, he could do little, for the citizens and their enemies could hardly see who was who in the narrow streets. Morning broke, and many a struggle took place in different parts of the town. The king was in the hottest of the fight. He was wounded by a javelin (a short spear), and was about to strike back at the man who injured him, when a large tile fell upon his neck and severely stunned him. The tile was thrown by an old woman. She had seen from a housetop that her son was in danger (for it was he who wounded Pyrrhus), and she hastened to save her son's life. Some men ran up and cut off the king's head. This was 272 B.C. So he never was able to "take his ease, eat, drink, and be merry." And if he had spent as much labor in useful work (say building, or ploughing, or sandal-making), what a good workman he might have become!

THE LAST OF THE GREEKS

"HERE, you fellow, come and chop this wood for my hearth-fire!"

The Greek lady was speaking to a tall, broad-shouldered man who had just come to the door of her house.

"Yes, madam, certainly," he said, and, throwing off his cloak, he began to cleave the wood which she pointed out to him. When the lady's husband arrived he was much surprised.

"Why, my friend," he cried, "what is the meaning of this?"

"You see, I am so ugly that your wife thought I was a slave, and bade me help her in the kitchen."

The master laughed.

"Well," he said, "come to supper now, for you have earned it."

The mistress felt rather confused when the tall man, whose name was Philopœmen (*Fil-o-pe´ -men*), 253–182 B.C., sat at her table as chief guest. He was General of the Achæan League, of which I have told you in a previous story, and she had mistaken him for one of his own servants!

Not only was he tall; he was also very strong and active. He was so fond of work that he often went out to his estate near the city of Megalopolis (Meg-a-lo-po-lis—Great City), and toiled in the fields for hours with the ploughmen or in the vineyards. Being fond also of horses and of war, he spent much time in training steeds for cavalry, and in buying and testing swords, spears, etc. When he took walks in the country with his friends, his thoughts were often of battles. He would say:

"Suppose one army was on the hill among those rocks, and suppose another army was posted on the opposite bank of this river, which would be in the better position?"

And so on. Besides this, he was a magistrate, and would sit in a court, hearing cases of quarrel and evil-doing that came before him. And when he rested in his house after the business of the day, he turned over his books, and chatted with his comrades about wisdom (or philosophy) and the poetry of Homer.

He joined his army with that of the King of Macedonia against the Spartans. The king told Philopœmen to wait with his horsemen at a certain spot until he saw a piece of red cloth lifted up on the end of a spear. Then he could charge with all his might. The noise of battle went on for some while, and Philopœmen waited and waited, until a troop of the enemy had pressed forward and caused terror among the Macedonians. Then he could wait no longer, but, with a shout, he led his horsemen to the onset, and they drove off the attacking force. Leaping from his horse, he ran on by himself, so eager was he to come at the foe. The ground was soft and boggy, and he slipped; and a dart from the enemy pierced the flesh of both his legs. He called to a companion to draw out the dart, and then he hobbled on, calling to his side to follow. With a big cheer they rushed, and the foe fled.

The king asked his officers why they had charged before he gave the order?

"We could not help it, for a young man from Megalopolis began the forward movement, and we were obliged to follow."

"That young man," replied the king, smiling, "has behaved like a tried captain. He knew the right moment to strike."

Even when there was no war, Philopœmen did much to practise young Greeks for battle. He persuaded them to wear suits of armor which covered them from head to foot, and taught them how to manage horses.

"If any of you," he said, "have gold and silver wine-cups and dishes, take them to the armor-makers, and let them use the metal to adorn your shields and breastplates and bridles."

And the young men did so.

In a battle against the Spartans, Philopœmen met the captain of the enemy, a tyrant, trying to cross a ditch on horseback. The steed was just struggling up the bank of the ditch, when Philopœmen thrust his spear into the tyrant's body and slew him. Not long afterward, when many Greeks were assembled at the public games, Philopœmen held a review of his troops, and his young men, marching by in scarlet jackets, were much admired. Just as their leader walked into the theatre, where the sports were being held, a musician was striking the strings of a lyre and singing:

"The palm of liberty for Greece I won."

The people shouted loudly, for they thought the words just fitted the brave Philopœmen. He did his best to keep the different Greek republics friendly with one another, and at the same time friendly with the strong kings of Macedon in the north; for he thought that was the wisest plan for making Greece orderly and happy. At last he got the Spartans also to join the Achæan League, and this saved Sparta from further war—at least, for a time. So the Spartans sent messengers to Philopœmen's house to thank him and to offer him a gift of gold. They came back and said they had not liked to give it him, for he seemed so honest a man that they did not think he would care to accept money for doing his duty to the liberty of Greece.

So another messenger was sent; but, though he dined at Philopœmen's house, he did not dare to mention the gold.

The same man was sent a second time, and still kept silence.

A third time he went, and then spoke: "Sir, I beg your pardon, but—ah!—well, I beg your pardon for naming the subject, but—would you care to take a—a—a—present from Sparta?"

Philopœmen thanked him, and would take nothing.

When he was seventy years old he was elected general of the League for the eighth time.

He lay at Argos, sick of a fever, when he heard that the city of Messene had broken away from the League. At once he rose from his bed, collected a body of cavalry, and met the enemy on the hills. A troop of five hundred men came to the aid of the foe, and his horsemen retired. Philopœmen was left alone. The enemy rode round and round and shouted and threw darts, but dared not come too near the old warrior. His horse stumbled among the crags, and he lay stunned. When he came to himself they bound his hands behind his back, and led him to the city. The Messenians beheld this famous captain led through their streets like an evil-doer, and some of them pitied him and some shed tears. He was put in a cell that had no light in it, nor had it a door, for it was closed by a huge block of stone.

As Philopœmen lay in this dungeon, covered with a cloak, he could not sleep. His thoughts kept going back to his wars, to Greece, and to his capture.

A light flashed in the dark cell. By the prisoner's bedside stood a man holding a lamp in one hand and a cup in the other. The cup contained poison. Philopœmen quite understood. He knew he must drink. When he had taken the cup, he asked:

"What became of my cavalry? Did they escape?"

"Yes," said the jailer; "they nearly all escaped."

The prisoner nodded his head as if much pleased.

"Thou bringest good tidings," he answered, "and I am not so unhappy as I should have been if I had not had this news."

So saying, he drank the poison, and lay down again. Presently he was dead.

When the news of his death was spread abroad there was a sound of grief in all the land. Many men gathered together in an army, and they marched upon the false city of Messene and entered it, and seized all the men who had had any part in the death of the general of the League.

His body was burned, and the ashes were placed in a pot or urn, and carried in a procession to his native city. First walked foot-soldiers wearing crowns of leaves and flowers, in memory of the victories which the dead patriot had gained. Then came his son carrying the urn, which was adorned with ribbons and garlands. Last appeared the horsemen in grand array. The people of the towns and villages on the way to the Great City crowded to the wayside, and raised mournful cries for the leader whom they had lost.

Soon the land of Greece was to fall into the power of the Romans. And when men thought of the noble general, and how there seemed no one as brave and good as he to stand up for the freedom of the country, they gave him a name which was beautiful and yet sad. They said that Philopœmen was "the last of the Greeks."